National Gun Association

History, Constitution and By-Laws

Trap-Shooting Rules, Tournament Programmes of the National Gun Association

National Gun Association

History, Constitution and By-Laws
Trap-Shooting Rules, Tournament Programmes of the National Gun Association

ISBN/EAN: 9783337162818

Printed in Europe, USA, Canada, Australia, Japan

Cover: Foto ©ninafisch / pixelio.de

More available books at **www.hansebooks.com**

History,
Constitution and By-Laws,
Trap-Shooting Rules,
Tournament Programmes

—OF—

THE NATIONAL GUN ASSOCIATION,

Organized—New Orleans, La., February 10, 1885.
Incorporated—Covington, Ky., March 4, 1885.

INCLUDING

The National Corps of Commissionaires,
The National Gun Corps, etc., etc.

PRICE, **10** CENTS.

OFFICE:
CINCINNATI, OHIO.

Copyrighted, 1885, by The National Gun Association.

THE
National Gun Association.

TABLE OF CONTENTS.

	PAGES.
Preface.	3
History: First Meeting	5
" Second "	8
List of First Vice-Presidents	9
" Second "	11
The Articles of Incorporation	13
The Constitution and By-Laws.	15
The National Gun Corps	26
The National Corps of Commissionaires.	28
The Trap Shooting Rules	30
Gun Clubs—Article on	43
Comments of Prominent Parties.	47
Clay Pigeon and Wing Shooting—Article on.	57
Scores at the First International Tournament, 1884	60
Scores and Guns at the Second International Tournament, 1885	67
The Annual July Telegraph Match.	72
Tournament Programme	73
The American Sportsman's Directory.	

SPECIAL NOTICE.

The subscriptions to the capital stock can now be made, payable in full at the time of subscription, or can be made payable as follows: 10 per cent. at time of subscription, and thereafter in monthly installments of 20 per cent. payable on the first of each ensuing month to the Treasurer of the Association if one share only be subscribed, or 10 per cent. if more than one share is subscribed; scrip receipts shall be issued therefor, the shares not being issued until the full value is received.

Any stockholder neglecting or refusing to pay an installment in whole or in part when required, the President and Directors may sell or dispose of such stock, and after deducting the expenses of such procedure, shall pay over to such stockholder any excess which may remain.

All stock of the Association is unassessable. Stockholders are guaranteed free from any liability whatever.

Parties desiring so to do, can join as members without subscribing to stock (or when the latter is all taken). by payment of $5.00 initiation fee (in monthly installments of 20 per cent. if preferred).

The National Gun Association Badge can be ordered from the Secretary now. Prices: In Bronze, 50 cents; in Silver, $1.25; in Gold, $10.00. Send stamp for the mailing of same in addition.

The Secretary of the Association will take charge of a New York office on and after May 20th, where he will be joined by Capt. A. H. Bogardus about June 1st.; they will then direct their efforts towards forming a large New York City Gun Club, under the auspices of the Association and under the name of

THE BOGARDUS GUN CLUB

Whose main objects it will be to secure suitable club rooms and shooting grounds, and otherwise similar to this Association.

With the view of centralizing and promoting the friendly rivalry between the most distant shooters it is proposed on the course of time, to divide the same geographically into four sections, viz: the "East" with the New York City as a center; the "West" with Chicago as a center; the "South" with Louisville or Nashville as a center; the "Pacific Coast" with San Francisco as a center; in each of which cities it will be the endeavor of the Association, to form a grand Gun Club, with (at least one of) which, each member of the Association will be identified.

Stock certificates are now ready for delivery to those who have paid in full, and members' certificates, to those who have paid their annual dues.

Address all communications to care Box 1292, Cincinnati, O.

PREFACE.

IF there is any one amusement, more than another, that should be placed upon a National footing, it is that of the Gun. This for various reasons: 1. In that it is conducive to health, it being essentially an out-door amusement. To be a good shot requires temperance, both in liquors and tobacco, and regularity of living; one must cultivate control of the nerves, quickness of the eye, and generally correct functions of the brain powers. 2. In that it is conducive to the military strength of the country, taking the place of the forced military service, in time of peace, of foreign governments. A man who is familiar with the use of the shotgun, is more than half a trained soldier.

It is broadly claimed, that if this subject be properly presented to the notice of the public, thousands of citizens, who are now utterly indifferent, will lend their support and active coöperation to placing this sport upon a broad National basis. How can this best be accomplished? No better plan can be suggested than that of encouraging The National Gun Association, whose objects and history are fully set forth in the ensuing pages. All reputable citizens are invited to join the same (whether sportsmen or not) upon the basis indicated in the Constitution. The attention of those not now interested in "the Gun," is especially invited to Articles XVI and XVII of the Constitution, and the explanatory articles thereon embodied herewith.

One of the great advantages of such an Association as this for Tournament purposes is, that it enables the Executive Committee to exclude all objectionable characters from participating therein. As Tournaments have been managed in the past few years, there was no central authority to exercise any discrimination in this regard, and therefore many shooters have abstained from attending same, who now will cheerfully do so.

A careful study of these pages will convince any unprejudiced mind that the objects of the Association are worthy the active support of all.   Very respectfully,

THE NATIONAL GUN ASSOCIATION,
Box 1292, *Cincinnati*, *O.*

HISTORY

OF THE

NATIONAL GUN ASSOCIATION.

[EXTRACTS FROM THE SECRETARY'S RECORD.]

IN pursuance to an informal call, the sportsmen in attendance at the Second International Clay-Pigeon Tournament, assembled at the office of Richard Rhodes (gun store), 55 St. Charles street, New Orleans, La., at 8 P. M., February 10, 1885, for the purpose of organizing a National Association. The meeting was formally organized by the election of Captain A. M. Aucoin, of New Orleans, La., as chairman *pro tem.*, and J. E. Bloom, of Cincinnati, Ohio, secretary *pro tem.* There were present in person —

Capt. A. M. Aucoin..New Orleans.	W. L. Davis..........Boston, Mass.
Wm. Mayronne, " "	H. L. Baker.........Natchez, Miss.
A. Cardona, Jr., " "	H. A. Penrose...San Angela, Tex.
John C. Curry, " "	Joseph Dils...Parkersburg, W. Va.
C. M. Stark..N. Dunbarton, N. H.	A. W. West, " "
John S. Snedeker..Brooklyn, L. I.	W. C. Lefell.........Springfield, O.
F. S. Parmelee......Omaha, Neb.	Dr. L. E. Russell, " "
A. Bandle...............Cincinnati.	W. B. Ralston........Blue Ball, O.
H. E. Peters, "	W. L. Colville......Pittsburgh, Pa.
H. McMurchy, "	E. E. Stubbs.....Gainesville, Ark.
J. E. Bloom, "	W. F. Summerson....Stanton, Va.
T. Gastright, "	W. Ackerman..............Lima, O.
B. Teipel, "	W. H. Bradley.......Bradford, Pa.
John A. Ruble....Ellendale, Dak.	C. E. Verges.............Lowell, O.
Geo. Essig ....Plattsburg, Mo.	J. A. R. Elliott.....Grenola, Kan.
Andy Meaders...Nashville, Tenn.	J. W. Campbell, " "
O. R. Dickey........Boston, Mass.	M. F. Cook.......Hartford, Conn.
D. Kirkwood, " "	Albert Erichson....Houston, Tex.
W. S. Perry, " "	H. W. Eager..Marlborough, Mass.
J. N. Frye, " "	A. H. Bogardus........Elkhart, Ill.
J. S. Sawyer, " "	L. Good................. New York.

Chas. Hallock...........New York.
C. H. Boulter..Cheyenne,Wy.Ter.
C. N. Brown...Fentonville, Mich.
L. Rainey..........Jacksonville, Ill.
J. Z. Scott,   "   "

Chas. E. Strawn..Jacksonville, Ill.
J. R. Stice,   "   "
Geo. B. Dougan...Leadville, Col.
A. E. Wakely .....Milford, Mich.,
And several others.

There were also present by proxy—

H. Durant, Algona Sportmen's Association...............Algona, Iowa.
R. B. Organ, President Chicago Shooting Club............Chicago, Ill.
J. M. Barbour, Pres't Louisville Sportsmen's Ass'n....Louisville, Ky.
Dr. L. E. Russell, Pres't Central Ohio Shooting Ass'n..Springfield, O.
E. S. Holmes, Pres't Mich. Sportsmen's Ass'n...Grand Rapids, Mich.
C. P. Richards, Sec'y South Ills. Sportsmen's Ass'n.....DuQuoin, Ills.
Dr. C. H. Gerrish, Pres't New England Trap Shooter's Association,
.........Exeter, N. H.
Wm. G. Cooper, President Chatham Gun Club.........Savannah, Ga.
E. C. Farrington, President Willard Shooting Ass'n....Portland, Me.
W. B. Witherell, President Boston Gun Club.............Boston, Mass.
F. M. Gilbert, Game Warden 1st District Indiana....Evansville, Ind.
A. G. Fleischbein, Bellville Rod and Gun Club..........Bellville, Ills.
W. E. Limberg, Buckeye Gun Club.....................Cincinnati, Ohio.
Wm. M. Parker, Treasurer Elizabeth Gun Club.......Elizabeth, N. J.
C. A. Bragg, Manager Globe Shot Works.............Philadelphia, Pa.
J. C. Sherlock, Clifton Gun Club........................Cincinnati, Ohio.
John H. Law, President Cosmopolitan Gun Club...   "   "
Wm. Wagner, Capital City Gun Club................Washington, D. C.
R. W. Crabb, Secretary Highland Gun Club.........Uniontown, Ky.
Wash. A. Coster, East. Field Trial Club................Flatbush, N. Y.
E. L. Mills, Capital City Gun Club. ....Washington, D. C.

J. von Lengerke..New York City.
Geo. E. Reading..Flemington,N.J.
B. R. Buffham..Henrietta, Texas.
W. S. Pike.............Orwell, Vt.
Dr.W. H. Vincent..Montpelier,Vt.
John Whetstone.....Cincinnati, O.

F. L. Chamberlain..Cleveland, O.
J. F. Ives...........Meriden, Conn.
Arthur W. DuBray..Newport, Ky.
E. A. Crawford..Tallahassee, Fla.
F. J. C. Swift.....Falmouth, Mass.
C. W. Taylor.......Camden, N. J.

Upon motion of J. E. Bloom, of Cincinnati, seconded by Dr. Russell, of Springfield, O., the following resolution was unanimously adopted, viz:

Resolved, 1. That the sportsmen here assembled, do hereby organize themselves into a National Gun Association, and invite sportsmen and citizens throughout the country to join them in this movement; secondly, that this organization be duly incorporated according to law in the State of Kentucky, according to the general plan outlined in the prospectus heretofore issued, with such modifications as may be adopted at this meeting or any adjournment thereof, or by the Board of Directors thereafter; and, thirdly, that the secretary *pro tem.* be and is hereby instructed, to take the necessary legal steps to file and duly complete the requisite corporation papers and all other papers, books, proceedings, etc., required by law to duly carry out the foregoing clauses.

Upon motion of J. E. Bloom, seconded by Dr. L. E. Russell, of Springfield, O., the following resolution was unanimously adopted, viz:

Resolved, First, that the Constitution and By-Laws as read (a slightly changed copy of which can be found on the following pages) be and are hereby adopted by the National Gun Association; secondly, that the same be referred to a committee of five, on constitution and by-laws, for revision and report at the next or an ensuing meeting.

The chair then appointed for said committee of five the following:

J. E. Bloom..............Cincinnati.	James N. Frye..............Boston.
R. B. Organ................Chicago.	Dr. L. E. Russell...Springfield, O.
J. K. Renaud.........New Orleans.	

Upon motion duly made and seconded and unanimously carried, a committee of twenty on rules for all kinds of shooting at the trap, was appointed by the chairman, as follows:

Dr. L. E. Russell, Springfield, Ohio, Chairman.

C. M. Stark..N. Dunbarton, N. H.	John Whetstone.....Cincinnati, O.
D. Kirkwood.........Boston, Mass.	A. Bandle............ " "
R. B. Organ...........Chicago, Ill.	H. W. Eager.....Worcester, Mass.
A. Meaders.......Nashville, Tenn.	W. S. Perry...... " "
Capt. A. M. Aucoin..New Orleans.	J. R. Stice.........Jacksonville, Ill.
L. P. Chaudet........ " "	A. Hunter...............New York.
F. A. Cousin.......... " "	Albert Erichson.....Houston, Tex.
Capt. A. W. West, Parkersburg, W. Va.	J. N. Frye...........Boston, Mass.
	Capt. A. H. Bogardus, Elkhart, Ill.
A. W. Ackerman.........Lima, O.	W. H. Bradley, Bradford, Pa.

Upon motion duly made, seconded, and carried, the chairman appointed the following committee of three on selection of national badge:

        H. W. Eager................Worcester, Mass.
        W. L. Colville...............Pittsburgh, Pa.
        J. E. Bloom...................Cincinnati, O.

Upon motion of J. E. Bloom, seconded by H. W. Eager, the following motion was unanimously adopted:

Resolved, That the secretary *pro tem.* be requested to now duly open the subscription-books for the capital stock of the Association, and that he shall act as treasurer *pro tem.*, receipting for the 10 per cent. or more of the original subscription now made.

The secretary then formally opened the subscription-books, and reported that, together with subscriptions previously ordered, the total subscriptions already amounted to $900, of which about $150 had been paid at time of subscribing.

Upon motion duly made, seconded, and carried, it was

Resolved, That when this meeting adjourns, it shall adojurn to meet again at this office at 8 P. M. next Saturday, February 14; and, secondly, that subscribers to the capital stock alone, be then and thereafter allowed to vote on any question which may be submitted; and, thirdly, that when we finally adjourn from New Orleans, we adjourn to meet again at Cincinnati, O., May 5 to 10.

Upon motion duly made, seconded, and carried, it was

Resolved, That the minutes of this meeting be duly included in the minutes of the Association when incorporated.

Upon motion of Capt. A. H. Bogardus, duly seconded and carried, it was

Resolved, That traps No. 2 and 4 be changed to throw left half quartering and right half quartering respectively, instead of the reverse as heretofore.

SECOND MEETING.

Pursuant to adjournment the National Gun Association members assembled at 55 St. Charles street, New Orleans, at 8 P. M., Feb. 14, with the following members present:

J. R. Stice..........Jacksonville, Ill.
W. H. Bradley.......Bradford, Pa.
J. C. Linneman......   "   "
D. Kirkwood.........Boston, Mass.
J. S. Sawyer........   "   "
J. N. Frye..........   "   "
C. M. Stark.....Winchester, Mass.
C. N. Brown...Fentonville, Mich.
Capt. A. H. Bogardus..Elkhart, Ill.
W. Ackerman..............Lima, O.
Dr. W. F. Carver.....New Haven, Conn.
Dr. L. E. Russell...Springfield, O.
J. E. Bloom..........Cincinnati, O.
C. E. Bardwell....Tekamah, Neb.
W. S. Perry......Worcester, Mass.
F. L. Chamberlain...Cleveland, O.
J. Leicht..............Liberty, Tex.
E. T. Owens........Natchez, Miss.
And numerous others.

Present by proxy, in addition to the proxies at first meeting, as indicated above:

F. W. Siefert......Nashville, Tenn.	W. H. Skinner......Waseca, Minn.
W. E. Watkins... " "	S. McDowell........Natchez, Miss.
J. L. Breese........New York City.	H. L. Palmer...Providence, R. I.
James Wood..........Cleveland, O.	J. W. Watson....Sacramento, Cal.
J. E. Riley......Kansas City, Mo.	C. A. Kimball...Ward Hill, Mass.
A. T. White........Tekamah, Neb.	Thos. P. Greger..Philadelphia, Pa.
Dr. H. H. Hurlburt..Ogden, Utah.	Geo. Lawrence..........New York.
W. D. Howe......... " "	Geo. D. May.....New Orleans, La.
A. C. Smith.......... " "	Henry Wurzbach........New York.
H. G. Doon.......... " "	J. H. Gates........Hartford, Conn.
W. R. Curtis......Fernandina, Fla.	

The chairman *pro tem.*, Captain A. M. Aucoin, sent a letter of regrets, being absent on account of the illness of a relative calling him out of the city. Dr. Russell, of Springfield, Ohio, was made chairman *pro tem*. The minutes of the previous meeting were read. Upon motion of W. S. Perry, of Worcester, seconded by J. R. Stice, of Jacksonville, Ill., the same were unanimously approved.

Upon motion of J. E. Bloom, seconded by Aug. Ackerman, of Lima, Ohio, and Captain A. H. Bogardus, the following resolutions were unanimously adopted, viz:

First. That residents of the British Provinces of North America, and of Mexico, be eligible for membership in this Association under the same conditions as residents of the United States.
Secondly. That Dr. N. Rowe, editor of the *American Field*, Chicago, C. E. Reynolds, editor of the *Forest and Stream*, New York, and L. C. Bruce, editor of the *Turf, Field and Farm*, New York, be and are hereby elected honorary life members of this Association; and,
Thirdly. That the chairman appoint a committee on organization, one for each State and Territory in the United States, whose duty shall be that of First Vice-presidents, provided for in the Constitution and By-laws.

The following committee was then appointed:

Alabama..............Judge Randolph.... ......Montgomery.
Arkansas . ...Geo. Read..................Sunnyside.
California..............J. K. Orr..................San Francisco.
Colorado ....Geo. B. Dougan......... .Leadville.
Connecticut...........C. M. Spencer.............Windsor.
Delaware..............E. Van Cullen..............Delaware City.
Florida.................E. A. Crawford..........Tallahassee.
Georgia.................Wm. F. Cooper..........Savannah.
Illinois..................R. B. Organ..............Chicago.

Indiana..................Edward Voris..........Crawfordsville.
Iowa......................Walter Chambers......Davenport.
Kansas....................F. A. White..........Topeka.
Kentucky.................J. M. Barbour.........Louisville.
Louisiana.................A. M. Aucoin..........New Orleans.
Maine.....................Col. E. C. Farrington. Portland.
Massachusetts............C. M. Stark........... Winchester.
Maryland.................E. A. Sharretts........Baltimore
Michigan.................E. S. Holmes..........Grand Rapids.
Minnesota ....W. H. Skinner........Waseca.
Mississippi..............D. N. Hebron..........Vicksburg.
Missouri..................R. W. Main............Fulton.
Nebraska.................F. S. Parmelee........Omaha.
Nevada...................Samuel King..........Austin.
New Hampshire........Dr. C. H. Gerrish...Exeter.
New Jersey...............Al. Heritage...........Jersey City.
New York................J. P. Fisher............Buffalo.
North Carolina.........J. W. Jordan..........Asheville.
Ohio......................Al. Bandle............Cincinnati.
Oregon...................W. Lang Chapman...Portland.
Pennsylvania............W. H. Bradley.........Bradford.
Rhode Island............E. W. Tinker..........Providence.
South Carolina..........T. E. Gibbes..........Columbia.
Tennessee................A. Meaders............Nashville.
Texas....................Albert Erichson.......Houston.
Vermont.................Dr. W. H. Vincent...Montpelier.
Virginia..................S. R. White...........Norfolk.
West Virginia...........Capt. A. W. West....Parkersburg.
Wisconsin................J. W. Phillips..........Chippewa Falls.
Canada...................J. E. Robertson.......Toronto.
New Mexico............J. W. Virgin...........Marcial.
District of Columbia...Wm. Wagner..........Washington.
Dakota...................John A. Ruble........Ellendale.
Utah......................W. D. Howe..........Ogden.
Wyoming................Paul Bergerson........Cheyenne.
Washington.............Mr. Hardy............Seattel.
Montana................F. Gilbert.............Butte.

Upon motion of Perry, of Worcester, seconded by Bradley, of Bradford, it was resolved that the last-named committee be increased from one to five, in the larger States, and that a number of workers at large be appointed.

The following additional workers were appointed, with the title and duties of Second Vice-Presidents, provided for in the Constitution and By-Laws.

Workers at Large—Capt. A. H. Bogardus, Dr. W. F. Carver, Dr. N. Rowe, Chicago; L. C. Bruce, New York; C. E. Reynolds, New York; S. A. Tucker, Meriden, Conn.
California—J. W. Watson, Sacramento; E. T. Allen, San Francisco.
Connecticut—M. F. Cook, Hartford; E. A. Folsom, Windsor; J. J. Phelps, New Haven.
Florida—W. R. Curtis, Fernandina.
Georgia—M. R. Freeman, Macon.
Illinois—C. P. Richards, Du Quoin; Henry Miller, Chicago; J. R. Stice, Jacksonville.
Indiana—Frank Gilbert, Evansville; Max Lade, Fort Wayne.
Iowa—H. Durant, Algona; W. E. Vernon, Oskaloosa.
Kansas—J. A. R. Elliott, Grenola; Max Schmelzer, Leavenworth.
Kentucky—R. W. Crabb, Uniontown; A. W. Du Bray, Newport; Dr. Van Antwerp, Mt. Sterling; J. O. Barbour, J. Griffith, Louisville.
Louisiana—Folsom Bros., A. Cardona, Jr., New Orleans.
Massachusetts—H. W. Eager, Marlborough; J. F. Fottler, Jr., D. Kirkwood, Boston; W. S. Perry, Worcester; O. R. Dickey, J. N. Frye, Boston.
Maryland—E. A. Colston, C. R. Pue, Baltimore.
Michigan—Jno. E. Long, Detroit.
Minnesota—E. A. Zimmerman, St. Paul.
Mississippi—E. T. Owens, S. McDowell, Natchez.
Missouri—J. E. Riley, Kansas City; D. T. Morton. Moberly.
New Jersey—Geo. E. Reading, Flemington; W. M. Parker, Elizabeth; Clarence W. Taylor, Camden.
New York—J. Von Lengerke, J. L. Breese, H. Wurzbach, C. J. Curry, G. W. Wade, New York; Wash. A. Coster, Flatbush; Geo. Barker, Niagara Falls; Geo. C. Luther, Syracuse; J. S. Snedeker, Brooklyn; Z. Stamm. Allentown; Fred. Tomkins, Stony Point; S. G. LeValley, Buffalo.
Ohio—F. L. Chamberlain, James Wood, Cleveland; John Bour, Canton; H. McMurchy, H. F. Robinson, Cincinnati; C. E. Verges, Lowell; J. Ritty, Dayton; A. Bellamy, Toledo; W. C. Leffel, Springfield.
Pennsylvania—C. A. Bragg, T. P. Greger, Philadelphia; J. Palmer

O'Neil, W. L. Colville, Pittsburgh; C. W. Babcock, Meadville.
J. C. Lineman, Bradford.
Texas—B. R. Buffham, Henrietta; H. A. Penrose, San Angela; W. D. Kimball, Clarendon.
Washington, D. C.—E. L. Mills.
Rhode Island—H. L. Palmer, Providence.
Tennessee—W. D. Mallory, Memphis; W. E Watkins, Nashville.
Vermont—N. S. Brockway, Bellows Falls; W. L. Pike, Orwell.
Virginia—W. F. Summerson, Stanton.

Upon motion duly made, seconded and carried, the following offer of Captain A. H. Bogardus, of Elkhart, Illinois, was accepted: Captain A. H. Bogardus offered to donate to the National Gun Association "The Bogardus Cup, won by him in England, in June, 1878, in a match against C. Pennell; stakes $3,000; conditions, one hundred single pigeons, thirty yards rise. Said cup is to be offered by the National Gun Association, to be shot for (and is to be known as "The Bogardus Cup") at every tournament held under the auspices of the National Gun Association in the ensuing two years. Conditions, fifty single clay pigeons, twenty-five double clay pigeons. National Gun Association rules to govern. Other conditions to be fixed by the Executive Committee.

Upon motion of J. N. Frye, of Boston, duly seconded and carried, a vote of thanks was given Captain A. H. Bogardus.

The Committee on Rules, per Dr. L. E. Russell, chairman, reported the trap-shooting rules, which were duly adopted, subject to revision by the executive committee; said rules, properly codified, and with various additions and changes, as adopted by the Executive Committee of the Association, will be found in the ensuing pages. The principal point of debate in regard to the rules, was the Winner's Handicap Rule, which was finally adopted upon motion of J. C. Lineman, of Bradford, Penn., seconded by C. E. Bardwell, of Tekamah, Neb. This, for the reason that without such a rule, the great majority of amateur shooters, though present on the grounds, would refuse to enter sweepstake matches with the few best shots of the country, as was fully demonstrated during the past week of the Second International Clay Pigeon Tournament.

The Committee on Badges, per H. W. Eager, chairman, reported, recommending the adoption of a design for a National Badge, from Tiffany & Co., New York, which was duly adopted. The same in bronze will cost fifty cents; in silver, $1.25, and in gold $10. Orders for same can be sent to the secretary.

There being no further business before the meeting, the same adjourned to meet again at Cincinnati, Ohio.

J. E. BLOOM, Secretary *pro tem.*

THIRD MEETING.

In pursuance of the resolution adopted by the assembled sportsmen, at New Orleans, La., Feb. 10, 1885, Mr. J. E. Bloom, of Cincinnati, O., the Secretary *pro. tem.*, employed W. H. Mackoy, Esq., Counselor at Law, of Cincinnati, O, and Covington, Ky., to duly prepare and file with the County Clerk at Covington Ky., February 28, 1885, the following:

Articles of Incorporation of The National Gun Association.

Know all men by these presents, That Jacob E. Bloom, Walter Irvine Jenckes, and Henry Franklin, have associated themselves and become an incorporated company, pursuant to the General Statutes of the State of Kentucky, for the purposes and upon the terms and conditions herein recited, under the corporate name of The National Gun Association.

1. The principal place of transacting the business of the said corporation shall be the city of Covington, Kentucky.

2. The general nature of the business to be transacted by the said corporation, shall be to organize shooting tournaments, to establish gun clubs throughout the United States, to promote shot-gun wing shooting, to adopt rules for all classes of shooting at the trap, to secure and manage game preserves, to protect and preserve birds, game and fish, to collect and preserve specimens of natural history, to publish reports of all matters of interest in connection with the objects of this association, and to promote and foster an interest in all lawful sports subsidiary to the main objects and business of this association.

3. The amount of the capital stock of the said corporation shall be the sum of five thousand dollars ($5,000) to be divided into shares of five dollars each, which shall be transferable only upon the books of the said corporation, by endorsement, and surrender of the certificate or certificates therefor, and no transfer of stock shall be made when the holder thereof is indebted to the corporation; but the company retains a lien upon the stock of each shareholder for all his liabilities to it. Five per cent. of the capital stock shall be paid in cash, prior to the first election of Directors of the corporation, and the remainder shall be paid at such times and in such installments as may be called for by the Board of Directors of the corporation.

4. The time of the commencement of the said corporation, shall be Wednesday, March 4, 1885, and it shall continue for the full term of twenty-five years, from and after that date, but it may be renewed and extended for another period, according to the law in such cases.

5. The affairs of the said corporation shall be managed by a Board of Directors, to consist of nine persons, who shall be stockholders therein, any three of whom shall constitute a quorum for the transaction of business.

The first election of Directors shall be held upon Wednesday, March 4, 1885, and the next election of Directors shall be upon the second Tuesday of January, 1886, and thereafter the election of Directors shall be held annually upon the second Tuesday of January of each and every year during the existence of the said corporation.

The Directors elected at any election shall hold office until their successors are elected and qualified, and in case of a failure for any reason to hold an election of Directors on the day fixed therefor, the Board of Directors of the corporation shall have the power to designate another day for the holding of an election.

6. The Board of Directors of the corporation shall elect from their number a President, Vice-President, General Manager, Secretary and Treasurer, any one or more of which offices, excepting those of President and Vice-President, may be held by the same person, and excepting also that neither the President nor Vice-President shall be or act as Secretary of the corporation.

It shall require from its Treasurer a bond in the sum of five thousand dollars, with good and sufficient security conditioned for the faithful performance of any and all duties that may be imposed upon or required of him by the By-Laws, rules and regulations of said Association, and that he will faithfully account for all money which may come into his hands as such Treasurer, and said Board may appoint such other agents, who need not be stockholders, as its business may require, and may demand of them, and of any of its officers, such bond as it may deem proper.

7. The highest amount of indebtedness or liability to which said corporation may at any time subject itself, shall not exceed two-thirds of its capital stock.

8. The private property of the stockholders in said corporation shall be exempt from the corporate debts thereof.

9. Vacancy or vacancies occurring in the Board of Directors may be filled by the remaining Directors, and the person or persons so chosen shall hold office until the next regular election of Directors, and until his or their successor or successors are elected and qualified.

10. The Directors of the corporation may hold meetings at such places as the business of the corporation may require.

11. The said corporation shall have the power to purchase, hold, lease and convey such real estate and erect such buildings as may be necessary for the business thereof.

12. Dividends may be declared annually or semi-annually, by the Directors, as they deem advisable, out of the earnings of the corporation.

13. The said corporation shall have such other power and privileges as are by the General Statutes and the laws of the State of Kentucky in such cases provided.

In testimony whereof, the said Jacob E. Bloom, Walter Irvine Jenckes and Henry Franklin, have hereunto set their hands this 28th day of February, 1885.

JACOB E. BLOOM,
WALTER IRVINE JENCKES,
HENRY FRANKLIN.

STATE OF KENTUCKY, } ss.
KENTON COUNTY.

I, John J. McCullom, Clerk of the County Court of Kenton County, Kentucky, do hereby certify that the foregoing Articles of Incorporation of the National Gun Association were on the 28th day of February, 1885, presented to me in my office, by Jacob E. Bloom, Walter Irvine Jenckes and Henry Franklin, the incorporators named therein, and acknowledged by them and each of them, to be their act and deed; and left for record. Whereupon the same and this certificate have been duly recorded in my office. Given under my hand, this 28th day of February, 1885.
J. J. McCOLLUM, Clerk.
By EDWARD RENZ, D. C.

ENDORSEMENT.

Acknowledged by Incorporators, Feb. 28th, 1885.
J. J. McCOLLUM, Clerk.
By E. RENZ, D. C.

Left for Record February 28, 1885. Recorded in Articles of Incorporation Book No. 2, Page 100.

In pursuance of the above, the stockholders duly assembled and elected a Board of Directors, who, amongst other acts, adopted the following "Constitution and By-Laws," and "Trap Shooting Rules," after referring same to the professional service of T. A. Logan, of Cincinnati, O. ("Gloan"), for revision, and due classification. The letter of the latter on the subject is as follows :

CINCINNATI, March 4, 1885.

J. E. BLOOM, Esq.,
(For the National Gun Association.)

MY DEAR SIR :—Enclosed find the Constitution and By-Laws. Taking these as they now stand, with the Rules, I must say, that I think you have an *inpregnable* record. There may be some little gaps, which will be disclosed when the machine gets working; it would be strange if there were not some such, for human foresight can not anticipate everything; but they can easily be remedied by the Board of Directors and Executive Committee from time to time, as occasion requires. Truly Yours,

GLOAN.

CONSTITUTION.

ARTICLE I.
Name.

This organization shall be known and designated by the name of "THE NATIONAL GUN ASSOCIATION."

ARTICLE II.
Capital Stock.

SEC. 1.—This organization is duly incorporated under the laws of Kentucky. There is no liability of the stockholder beyond the amount originally subscribed.

SEC. 2.—The capital stock is $5,000, divided into shares of $5 each.

SEC. 3.—Each share of stock subscribed, and upon which payment has been made as required under the laws of Kentucky, entitles the holder to one vote.

SEC. 4.—The transfer of stock may be made by any stockholder or his legal representative, subject to the laws of Kentucky, and such restrictions as the Board of Directors shall from time to time make and establish.

ARTICLE III.
Objects.

SEC. 1.—The main objects of the Association shall be :

The general nature of the business to be transacted by the said corporation shall be to organize shooting tournaments, to establish gun clubs throughout the United States, to promote shotgun wing shooting to adopt rules for all classes of shooting at the trap, to secure and manage game preserves, to protect and preserve birds, game and fish, to collect and preserve specimens of natural history, to publish reports of all matters of interest in connection with the objects of this Association, and to promote and foster an interest in all lawful sports, subsidiary to the main objects and business of this Association.

ARTICLE IV.
Board of Directors.

SEC. 1.—The affairs of the said corporation shall be managed by a Board of Directors, to consist of nine persons, who shall be stockholders therein, any three of whom shall constitute a quorum for the transaction of business.

SEC. 2.—The first election of Directors shall be held upon Wednesday, March 4, 1885, and the next election of Directors shall be upon the second Tuesday of January, 1886, and thereafter the election of Directors shall be held annually upon the second Tuesday of January, of each and every year during the existence of the said corporation.

SEC. 3.—The Directors elected at any election shall hold office until their successors are elected and qualified, and in case of a failure for any reason to hold an election of Directors on the day fixed therefor, the Board of Directors of the corporation shall have the power to designate another day for the holding of an election.

ARTICLE V.
Officers.

SEC. 1.—The Board of Directors of the corporation shall elect from their number a President, Vice-President, General Manager, Secretary and Treasurer, any one or more of which offices, excepting those of President and Vice-President, may be held by the same person, and excepting also that neither the President nor Vice-President shall be or act as Secretary of the corporation.

SEC. 2.—It shall require from its Treasurer a bond in the sum of five thousand dollars, with good and sufficient security, conditioned for the faithful performance of any and all duties that may be imposed upon or required of him by the by-laws, rules and regulations of said Association, and that he will faithfully account for all money which may come into his hands as such Treasurer, and said Board may appoint such other Agents, who need not be stockholders, as its business may require, and may demand of them, and of any of its officers, such bond as it may deem proper.

SEC. 3.—The Board of Directors shall also elect First Vice-Presidents, one for each State and Territory in the United States, selected from the shareholders of the Association. The duties and powers of all officers shall be such as is conferred on them by the Constitution and By-Laws.

SEC. 4.—They shall also elect additional officers, selected from the stockholders at large, whose duties shall be similar to the First Vice-Presidents', for the country at large, and whose title shall be Second Vice-Presidents.

SEC. 5.—The Directors shall also have power and authority to appoint such other officers under them as shall be necessary for transacting the business of said Association, and may allow them and all actively employed officers such salaries as they may judge reasonable; to ordain and establish such laws and regulations as may appear to them necessary for regulating and conducting the concerns of said Association, and not being contrary to, or inconsistent with this Constitution and By-Laws, and laws of the State of Kentucky, and of the United States; they shall keep full, fair and correct entries of their transactions, which shall at all times be open to the inspection of the stockholders, in the presence of, or upon order from the General Manager.

SEC. 6.—No member shall be eligible to the office of President for more than two consecutive terms.

ARTICLE VI.
The Executive Committee.

SEC. 1.— The Board of Directors shall appoint from among its members an

Executive Committee of three, of whom the General Manager shall be one, to whom shall be delegated all the duties and powers of the Board of Directors when not in session, excepting as qualified in this Constitution and By-Laws.

SEC. 2.—At any tournament held under the auspices of this Association, all the Directors shall be ex-officio members of the Executive Committee for same.

ARTICLE VII.
Annual Meetings.

SEC. 1.—The members of this Association shall hold an annual meeting at the principal office of the Association on the second Tuesday of January of each year, and such special meetings as may be called pursuant to the By-Laws. If the annual meeting shall not take place at the time fixed, it shall be held as soon after as convenient, and the officers and Directors whose terms have expired shall hold over until their successors are appointed.

SEC. 2.—The President and Directors may call a general meeting of the stockholders for any purpose relative to the affairs of the Association.

SEC. 3.—At no meeting of the Association shall any subject be introduced or discussed which does not relate directly to its affairs.

ARTICLE VIII.
Quorum of Stockholders' Meeting.

SEC. 1.—At any meeting of the Association, holders of one-tenth of the capital stock present in person or by proxy shall constitute a quorum, and a majority of votes present only is necessary for the election of any Director, or the transaction of any business of the Association.

ARTICLE IX.
Membership.

SEC. 1—Membership shall be divided into the following six different classes, viz.:

Class 1.—*Honorary Members.*—The Board of Directors, by unanimous vote, can confer Honorary Life Membership upon any one. The same shall be entitled to all privileges of Annual Members, with the exception of the right to vote or hold office, and they shall not have any interest in the property of the Association.

Class 2.—*Life Members.*—Every individual holder of five shares ($25) of stock shall be a Life Member of the Association, free from all other dues, entitled to all the privileges of Annual Members.

Class 3.—*Annual Members.*—Any reputable resident of the United States, of the British Provinces of North America, and of Mexico, can become an Annual Member of the Association (subject to the vote of the Board of Directors or Executive Committee). Initiation fee, $5; annual dues, $1, payable May 1. Any one holding an original share of the Association, viz., $5, need not pay any initiation fee to become a member; he becomes an Annual Member by paying $1 annually, though he does not lose his stock by failing to pay his annual dues, in which event he becomes an inactive stockholder merely. When the original shares are all subscribed, the initiation fee of $5, required from subsequent members, is forfeited when the annual dues are not paid.

Class 4.—*Club Membership.*—Clubs and Associations already organized, or which may be organized without any assistance from this Association, shall pay: initiation fee, $3 per member; yearly dues, $1 per Annual Member.

Class 5.—*Club Membership.*—Clubs organized under the auspices and aid of the Association shall pay: initiation fee, etc., same as Class 3.

Class 6.—*State Association or any sectional organization Membership.*—When organized and consisting of at least three clubs, shall pay : initiation fee, $2 per member ; yearly dues, $1 per Annual Member.

SEC. 2.—Any person giving his name, age, address and the name of the organization (if any) with which he is connected, shall, upon paying to the Secretary the initiation fee and yearly dues, become a member of the Association, subject to above vote, and any club or association giving a statement of the time of its organization, the name of its present officers, the number of members, and paying the prescribed fees to the Secretary, shall become a member, subject to above vote.

SEC. 3.—The President of the United States, the General commanding the Army of the United States, and also the Major and Brigadier Generals thereof, the Governors of the States and Territories of the United States, the Adjutant-General and Chief of Ordnance of the United States Army, and the Adjutant-General of the various States and Territories of the United States, shall be Honorary Life Members of this Association.

SEC. 4.—Whenever a gun club or association now organized, or which shall be formed in any of the States or Territories, shall join this Association as a body, the President thereof shall be an Honorary Life Member of the Association.

ARTICLE X.

Rights of Members.

SEC. 1.—Annual members only shall be allowed to shoot at tournaments held under auspices of this Association.

SEC. 2.—Annual members will be allowed to shoot at any tournament held under the auspices of any club or association receiving any prize or assistance from this Association in managing said tournament.

SEC. 3.—Annual members will be allowed to shoot at any tournament held under the auspices of a club or association which has been founded under the auspices of this Association.

SEC. 4.—Annual members will be allowed full privilege to use the principal office of this Association and of any club rooms, etc., which the latter may establish.

SEC. 5.—Annual members only, will be allowed to wear the badge of this Association, which shall entitle the wearer to enter the grounds, gratis, where any tournament is in progress under the auspices of this Association.

SEC. 6.—Annual members only, shall be entitled to the printed reports of this Association gratis, which shall embody the Constitution and By-Laws of this Association, the national shooting rules, latest legal decisions, announcements, etc.

SEC. 7.—Annual members only, will be allowed to appeal to the Committee on Grievances, on Rules and on Law, for the settlement of any and all controversies—thus obtaining the benefit of "a court of last resort," which shall interpret the shooting rules adopted by this Association, and whose decision shall be final.

SEC. 8.—Owners of capital stock only, shall be entitled to the annual dividends accruing from profits of tournaments, etc.

SEC. 9.—Owners of capital stock only, shall be entitled to vote at election of directors and at annual meetings.

SEC. 10.—No member shall be allowed to transfer his rights of membership, excepting holders of capital stock.

SEC. 11.—All rights and interests of a member in the property and privileges of the Association shall cease with the termination of his membership, excepting interests in the property by the holders of capital stock.

SEC. 12.—Associations or clubs being members shall be entitled to have the names and addresses of their officers for that year, and the scores made during the year at its two principal matches, to be certified as correct by its secretary, published in each annual report of this Association; and also

SEC. 13.—To receive the medal of this Association, for competition among its members, in such manner as it shall prescribe.

SEC. 14.—Any member having complaints or suggestions to make as to the management of the Association, must make them in writing to the Secretary, to be submitted to the Board of Directors.

SEC. 15.—No member shall take any property whatsoever belonging to the Association from its rooms or grounds, except on the authority of a resolution of the Board of Directors or Executive Committee.

SEC. 16.—Any member wishing to resign shall tender his resignation in writing to the Secretary.

ARTICLE XI.
Penalties.

SEC. 1.—Members in arrears for dues or fines, or any member who shall neglect to pay any indebtedness to the Association on demand, shall forfeit his or their membership (by majority vote of Board of Directors or Executive Committee) in the Association, and can not be reinstated in such membership except by vote of Board of Directors and payment of all arrears.

SEC. 2.—Any member who shall have violated any of the rules of the Association may be fined, by majority vote of the Board of Directors or Executive Committee; or any member whose conduct shall be pronounced by vote of the Board of Directors or Executive Committee to have endangered, or to be likely to endanger, the welfare, interest, or character of the Association, shall forfeit his membership; but such vote shall not be taken without giving two weeks' notice to the offender of the charges made against him, and affording him an opportunity to be heard in his defense. No person so removed shall be eligible for membership unless his disability is removed by a similar vote.

SEC. 3.—Any member of the Board of Directors who shall in its opinion conduct himself in a manner seriously prejudicial to the interests of the Association may be removed from the Board of Directors at any stated meeting, provided the member accused shall have been at least ten days previously personally notified in writing, of the charges against him, and a hearing given him thereon at a stated meeting to be therein specified. But such removal can only be effected by the affirmative vote of at least two-thirds of all the members of the Board.

ARTICLE XII.
Dividends.

SEC. 1.—The President and Directors may declare such dividends of the profits of the business of the Association as they may deem warranted, provided that they shall not impair, nor in any way lessen the capital stock of the same. The dividends shall be made yearly, or semi-annually, and shall be paid to the stockholders within ten days thereafter, but no dividends shall be paid to any stockholder whose stock is delinquent.

ARTICLE XIII.
By-Laws, Rules, etc.

SEC. 1.—This Association shall have the power to make such By-Laws, Rules, and Regulations for its officers and members, and take such action for the protection of its property and the promotion of its objects, as may be deemed necessary and expedient.

SEC. 2.—The By-Laws may be altered at any regular meeting of the Board of Directors by a majority vote, notice in writing of the intended change having been given at the preceding regular meeting, but the operation of any By-Law may be suspended during a meeting by the same vote without notice.

ARTICLE XIV.
Seal and Badge.

SEC. 1.—The Board of Directors shall adopt a corporate seal for the Association; they shall also adopt a badge to be worn by members of the Association.

ARTICLE XV.
Altering Constitution.

SEC. 1.—This Constitution shall be changed only at an annual meeting, notice in writing or by publication having been given of the intended change, or such alteration and amendment may be made without previous notice by a unanimous vote of the stockholders present.

ARTICLE XVI.
The National Gun Corps.

SEC. 1.—Whenever the membership of the Association reaches two hundred, the Board of Directors shall, if in their discretion it is practical to do so, organize the members into a National Gun Corps. Such organization shall be upon the basis of the military systems of the United States; the members shall elect their own officers, and have the same privileges and duties as other volunteer military organizations. But there shall be no compulsion of members to join the same. It shall be purely voluntary. If organized, such corps, or the various subdivisions thereof, shall be subject to the control of the civil authorities, State and municipal, in time of danger, to suppress riot, insurrection, or other lawlessness, and in every way to protect life and property, and to maintain the public peace. Their head-quarters and drill-rooms shall be in the cities and large towns. Provided, however, that no service elsewhere than in their own communities shall be exacted of them without their express consent.

SEC. 2.—The Board of Directors may establish, from among its members, an Insurance Fund (Life and Accident) for the benefit of those members of the corps who may meet with any mishap, while in the performance of any duty pertaining to the corps.

ARTICLE XVII.
The National Corps of Commissionaires.

SEC. 1.—Whenever the Board of Directors deem it practical so to do, they shall organize, from amongst the members of the Association [who must also be members of the National Gun Corps, should the latter be organized as per Art. XVI], a National Corps of Commissionaires, whose object it shall be to obtain employment for its members, viz.: such as usually pertains to the office or work of "a commissionaire."

SEC. 2.—They shall establish Rules and Regulations to govern said Corps; and shall establish subdivisions in the various cities of the country.

SEC. 3.—They may, in their discretion, establish amongst the members a Sick Fund, a Life Insurance Fund, a Retiring (Old Age) Fund, and a "Savings Bank" System.

BY-LAWS.

ARTICLE I.
Board of Directors.

SEC. 1.—Meeting of Directors shall be held quarterly at the office of the Association on the second Tuesday of January, April, July, and October, at 2 o'clock P. M. Special meetings may be called by the President or General Manager, such calls specifying the object of the meeting. The first meeting of the Directors shall take place immediately after their election, for the purpose of electing officers and transacting necessary business.

SEC. 2.—In attending an annual meeting only, shall the necessary traveling expenses of the members of the Board of Directors be paid by the Treasurer.

Any member of the Board of Directors shall be entitled to the same privilege and remuneration as is allowed the Second Vice-Presidents as per Art. V. of these By-Laws.

SEC. 3.—In the absence of both President and Vice-Presidents from any meeting of the Association, any member present may be selected to preside.

SEC. 4.—The Board of Directors shall have charge of all the property, effects, and assets of the Association, excepting as qualified in Constitution and By-Laws, and shall have the management and control of the same, and exercise a general superintendence of its interests and affairs; they shall approve all necessary contracts and purchases in the name of the Association, which are necessary to carry out the provisions of this Constitution, excepting as qualified in the Constitution and By-Laws, but shall have no power to make the Association liable for any debt beyond the amount of money which shall at the time of contracting such debt be in the Treasurer's hands, and not needed for the discharge of prior debts or liabilities, or of those created by the Association. They shall have power generally to do all things which may be necessary for the proper management of the concerns of the Association.

SEC. 5.—Meetings of the Board of Directors and Stockholders shall be governed by the "Parliamentary Rules" as used in the United States House of Representatives.

SEC. 6.—The Board of Directors shall fix such additional Rules and Regulations as the objects of the Association shall require.

ARTICLE II.

Duties of President.

SEC. 1.—It shall be the duty of the President to preside at all meetings of the Association and of the Board of Directors, and to maintain order, enforce the rules and regulations, and to perform such other duties as usually pertain to the office of president of an association. He shall have the power, whenever he deems it necessary, to call special meetings of the Board of Directors at the principal office of the Association. And he shall call special meetings of the Association whenever directed so to do by holders of one-tenth of the stock thereof, and of the Board of Directors whenever directed by three of the members thereof, said notices to be in writing. He shall countersign all stock certificates, contracts, etc.

ARTICLE III.

Duties of Vice-President.

SEC. 1.—It shall be the duty of the Vice-President to perform all the duties of the President at, and during the absence of the latter, from the principal office of the Association.

ARTICLE IV.

Duties of First Vice-Presidents.

SEC. 1.—The duties of First Vice-Presidents shall be similar to those of Second Vice-Presidents, for the country at large; they shall be part of the permanent Committee on Organization.

ARTICLE V.

Duties of Second Vice-Presidents.

SEC. 1.—The Second Vice-Presidents shall constitute a Committee on Organization for their respective States and Territories, whose duty it shall be to promote the interests of the Association in their respective States and sections; to canvass the same for members, a commission being allowed them of ten per cent. of the membership fee (payable when the latter has been paid in full), for each member they may induce to join the Association. Their travelling expenses, incurred for the latter object, or in the interest of the Association, having previously been authorized by the General Manager, shall be duly paid by the Treasurer. At any tournament given under the auspices of the Association, they shall be ex-officio members of the Executive Committee for same.

ARTICLE VI.

Duties of General Manager.

SEC. 1.—The General Manager shall be the Chief Executive Officer to carry out the objects of the Association. He shall execute the orders of the Board of Directors and Executive Committee, and in the absence of the specific instructions of the latter in carrying out the objects of the Association, he is authorized to proceed as he deems best, but he shall incur no expenditure exceeding $50, without the authority of the Executive Committee or the Board of Directors. He shall receive such salary as the Board of Directors may annually fix. He shall appoint such subordinate officers as he deems requisite in managing any tournament. He shall appoint such subordinate assistants as he may deem requisite to assist in conducting the business of the Association, subject, however, to the approval of a majority of the Executive Committee or of the Board of Directors.

SEC. 2.—All the duties and powers of the Executive Committee when not in session, or when not accessible within reasonable time, shall be exercised and discharged by the General Manager. He shall have power, whenever he deems it necessary, to call meetings of the Board of Directors. He shall also make all contracts subject to the approval of the Executive Committee. He shall make all purchases, and report the same when made to the Secretary.

ARTICLE VII.

Duties of Secretary.

SEC. 1.—The Secretary of the Association shall notify each member of the Board of Directors of all its meetings, and each member of the Association of every meeting of the Association ; issue all other authorized notices to members; make and keep a true record of all meetings of the Directors, the Association and the Executive Committee; have custody of the books and papers and corporate seal of the Association, and conduct all correspondence, and give timely notice to the Directors at their regular meetings of all annual reports required to be made. He shall notify applicants for membership of their election, and perform such other duties as may appertain to the recording secretary of an association. He shall, in January of each year, make an inventory of the property of the Association, with the estimated value thereof. His books shall be open for inspection at both regular and special meetings of the Association.

SEC. 2.—He shall keep the books of the Association, including the books of the Treasurer, should the latter so elect, and balance the same up to the first days of June and December, and oftener, if required ; shall lay before the Directors, at their quarterly meetings, and at other times when required, a full statement of the condition of the Association ; may receive and collect money, and deposit the same with the Treasurer to the credit of the Association, and shall perform such other duties as may be required of him.

SEC. 3.—The Secretary shall keep the accounts of the members. He shall give notice to members in arrears, and shall make a special report of all members who are six months in arrears, that action may be taken thereon, as per Article XII. of the By-Laws.

SEC. 4.—He shall charge 25 cents for each new certificate issued in making transfers of stock.

SEC. 5.—He shall sign all stock and members' certificates and affix the corporate seal thereto, and shall receive such salary as the Board of Directors may fix.

SEC. 6.—He shall issue all Handicap Cards, Pigeon Cards, etc., provided for in the Trap Shooting Rules, and attend to such other duties as the Board of Directors may indicate.

ARTICLE VIII.
Duties of Treasurer.

SEC. 1.—The Treasurer shall receive all moneys and other assets of the Association, and be the custodian of the same. He shall be the fiscal agent of the Association, and shall make a detailed report of his accounts at every regular meeting, or whenever required to do so by a vote of the Association or the Board of Directors. He shall also make an annual report to the Association at its annual meeting. He shall pay all bills, taking receipts therefor where practicable, which shall be audited monthly or quarterly by the Executive Committee.

SEC. 2.—The Treasurer shall give bond in the sum of Five Thousand Dollars, with security to the Board of Directors, conditioned faithfully to account for and pay over all moneys which may come into his hands, and for the faithful performance of all the duties of his office. He shall receive such salary as the Board of Directors shall determine.

ARTICLE IX.
Duties of Executive Committee.

SEC. 1.—The Executive Committee shall have general supervision of the finances of the Association, with power to appoint and discharge all agents and employes, and to fix compensation of same. They shall from time to time credit all bills, examine the accounts of the Treasurer, and keep themselves informed of the financial condition of the Association. To this Committee shall be referred the Treasurer's reports, and all questions and propositions relating to finances, and no obligations of the Association beyond those necessary for current wants shall be made until the Committee have considered and reported upon the necessity and propriety of the plan proposed.

SEC. 2.—The Executive Committee may fix periods for its regular meetings, and may be convened upon the written demand of any member.

SEC. 3.—All the powers and duties of the Board of Directors not herein delegated to the officers or to other committees, shall be exercised and discharged during the recess of the Board by this committee.

SEC. 4.—Two members shall constitute a quorum.

SEC. 5.—They shall keep regular minutes of their proceedings, which shall be recorded in a book kept for that purpose in the office of the Association, which shall be reported to the Board of Directors after having previously been approved by the committee.

SEC. 6.—They shall take cognizance of all infractions of the By-Laws, Shooting Rules, conduct unbecoming a member, etc., in the intervals of Directors' meetings.

SEC. 7.—They shall select and procure the prizes offered by the Association.

SEC. 8.—All the acts of the Executive Committee shall be binding upon the Association, unless disapproved by the Board of Directors at a regular meeting.

SEC. 9.—They shall also act as a Committee on Grievances, Rules, etc., until special committees are provided therefor.

ARTICLE X.
Membership.

SEC. 1.—Whenever any person shall be proposed for Annual Membership, written application must be made to the Board of Directors, through the Secretary, subscribed by him, setting forth the name and place of residence of the person proposed (the initiation fee paid to the Secretary), and upon their majority vote, favoring his admission, the Secretary shall notify him of his election.

SEC. 2.—Honorary members may be elected upon their names being proposed and acted upon in the mode prescribed for annual members, a unanimous vote being required. They shall not be required to pay an initiation fee, and shall be entitled to all the privileges of active members, with the exception of the right to vote or to hold office, or to have any pecuniary interest in the property of the Association.

SEC. 3.—Non-members may be allowed the privileges of annual members, under such restrictions as may be fixed by the Board of Directors, Executive Committee, or General Manager.

SEC. 4.—It shall be the duty of members of the Association to conform to all requirements of the Constitution and By-Laws, Rules and Regulations.

SEC. 5.—Members shall notify the Secretary of any change of their residence or place of business.

SEC. 6.—New Members can, if they so elect, pay their membership fee ($5) in monthly installments of $1, paying the annual dues ($1) at the time of paying the first installment.

ARTICLE XI.
Resignation.

SEC. 1.—Any member may resign from the Association by giving notice in writing to the Secretary, but no resignation shall be accepted if the member be in arrears for dues or otherwise. Upon the acceptance of such resignation, all interest in the property of the Association of the member resigning, or in any manner ceasing to be a member, shall be vested in the Association, excepting as indicated in the Constitution.

ARTICLE XII.
Penalties.

SEC. 1.—Any member failing to pay his dues or fines shall be liable to expulsion, and when six months in arrears, his name shall be brought before the Executive Committee, or Board of Directors for such action as they may direct.

SEC. 2.—Any member of the Association may be expelled, forfeiting all rights in the property of the Association, for conduct unbecoming a gentleman, at any meeting of the Executive Committee or Board of Directors, upon a majority vote of the members present; provided any such member who may be charged with conduct deserving expulsion shall have fourteen days' previous notice of charges to be made against him at such meeting, together with a copy of the charges against him, at which meeting he may be present and meet the charges so preferred against him, and shall be entitled to be heard.

SEC. 3.—Any member causing any injury to the property of the Association shall have the same repaired, and should he neglect forthwith to do so, the Board of Directors or Executive Committee shall cause the same to be done, and direct the Secretary to charge the expense thereof to the offending member.

SEC. 4.—No game of any kind shall be played for money at any time in the Association rooms, under penalty of expulsion by the Executive Committee.

SEC. 5.—No member shall take any book or other property of the Association without permission of the Executive Committee or General Manager.

SEC. 6.—No Director shall divulge to persons not members of the Association any of its transactions.

SEC. 7.—All dues, fines and penalties shall be charged upon the books of the Secretary, and can only be remitted for cause shown, and at a meeting of the Board of Directors or Executive Committee.

SEC. 8.—Any member in arrears for dues or fines shall not be entitled to vote at an annual election.

ARTICLE XIII.
Residuary Powers.

SEC. 1.—All matters not particularly provided for in the Constitution or By-

Laws, shall be controlled by the Board of Directors or Executive Committee until specially passed upon by the Association at any meeting.

ARTICLE XIV.

Shooting Rules.

The Board of Directors shall appoint committees on shooting rules, and adopt shooting rules for all classes of shooting at the trap and for management of tournaments, which shall be submitted for the approval of members at the first annual meeting thereafter; and which can subsequently be amended only at future annual or other members' meetings.

ARTICLE XV.

Membership Pro Tem.

Until January 1, 1887, the Board of Directors shall, at their option, be authorized to allow any shooter, not a member of the Association, to participate in any single tournament given by the Association, or in any special contest, whether arranged by the Association or by others, and where the officers of this Association may be called upon to act in some capacity in connection therewith, whether as stake-holders, referees, or what not, upon payment of $2, by each contestant, to the treasurer of the Association, such contestants shall be known as "members pro tem," for said contests only, and shall be subject to like fines and expulsion, in accordance with the foregoing articles, rules, etc.

ARTICLE XVI.

Upon the appearance of a quorum at the time appointed for any meeting of the Board or of the Association, the meeting shall be called to order, and proceed in the following

ORDER OF BUSINESS.

1. Calling roll of members present.
2. Reading minutes of last meeting and of previous minutes not passed on.
3. Report from officers, standing and select committees.
4. Motions and resolutions.
5. Election of members.
6. General business. Adjournment.

THE NATIONAL GUN CORPS.

Article XVI of the Constitution embodies a feature which will doubtless appear new to most readers, but it is really a revival of an old institution, viz: the organization into volunteer companies, of those who use a shot-gun [for hunting purposes or for amusement at an artificial target]. and for the purpose of aiding the civil authorities, in their own communities, in times of wild riot and lawlessness. At the present day such an organization serves a double purpose: First: it will prove to the public, who now take no interest whatsoever in the gun, and who, if anything, are inclined to look with suspicion and distrust upon its present use, that an additional and meritorious interest attaches thereto, and for the reason that it thus becomes a useful public servant in time of danger and of its need; and hence thousands of public-spirited citizens will take an interest in its development, will join the association, will encourage and attend its tournaments, and induce their friends to do likewise, who otherwise would remain the passive, indifferent spectators they now are. And secondly, it will elevate the sportsmen themselves, not only by bringing a new and worthy element into their ranks, but also and more especially by adding a noble, patriotic purpose to the present objects of amusement at the trap and in the field only.

The political and economical character of our American cities is such that they will ever be subject to times of riot. The doctrine of the communist is a growing one. The distance between the rich and the poor, the capitalist and the laborer is spreading more and more. The reckless political agitation we see from year to year, adds fuel to the flames, by bringing about a corrupt political state of affairs, which widens these distances, and which leads to periods of excitement, and of disrespect for the power and the justice of the law, and which results in violent outbursts of a misled populace, detrimental to all law and order and most injurious to the very instruments themselves, who thus vent the popular fury. Such a state of affairs occurred in Cincinnati in 1884, resulting in the killing of about 56 and the wounding of about 200 misled enthusiasts, and the destruction of nearly $2,000,000 of property and innumerable and invaluable court records; all of which could doubtless have been avoided, had the civil authorities had, at their disposal, one hundred organized expert sportsmen armed with the shot-gun and revolver only. There are mobs and mobs. The above one, was not composed of vagabonds and outcasts, but rather of "misled respectable citizen enthusiasts," aggravated by the previous failure of the judiciary to perform its work justly, and further excited by the well-meant, but heated condemnatory addresses in public meeting of many of Cincinnati's best citizens. Such a mob should not have been plowed down and slaughtered with rifles, which kill; but should rather have been scattered with "buck-shot," which only wound. This is not a despotic government; it is not a Russian or a Napoleonic Empire, where "the people" are regarded as so many "cattle," fit only to be slaughtered; but it is a Republic "for the people, of the people and by the people," and where "the people" are regarded as the peers of each other, and where it is the object to make every man feel, that he has some interest at stake in the preservation of the government, of which he is a part, and where it is and should always be an object to *persuade* the people to do what is right not with the cannon-ball, a la Napoleon, but with lesser means which will not kill. What cared Napoleon, whether he killed or sacrificed one or a thousand. His aim was not a Republic, but an Empire. We, on the other hand, do *not* want an Empire, but a Republic; hence his methods must not be our methods; for when you kill once, you engender a feeling of bitterness and of revolt in the multitude, which only leads to additional repetitions of the same scene on a larger and larger scale, until finally a despotism of some nature results, as a lesser evil between two. Hence it should be the policy of the authorities to employ such a force in dispersing mobs of the above character, as will not kill and will not therefore undermine the very pedestals of the Republic. Such a force is at hand in the "shot-gun," if it be but organized in the general manner outlined in Art. XVI. Let sportsmen, those who now own guns, give it their support, but above all, let all good citizens, who appreciate the force of the above argument, give their support to this association, by joining it as contributing members.

The National Corps of Commissionaires.

Many sportsmen will doubtless now ask; "But how are we individually to be otherwise benefitted thereby?"

Primarily, by making large tournaments a financial success, so that the "guarantees" therein can be increased from year to year, and the number of attendants and participants likewise increased. But there is a subsidiary benefit to accrue to a large minority of the members, who may desire to avail themselves of the same, viz: through the organization of The National Corps of Commissionaires, as outlined in Art. XVII, and patterned after the Corps of Commissionaires as it now exists in various European cities. The attention of the visitor to the latter is at once called to the neatly, plainly uniformed Commissionaire, whom he finds at his monetary service, whether it be as a faithful messenger or courier, a reliable watchman, an accurate clerk, a trustworthy nurse, an expert guide or any other service, whether temporary or permanent, for which the central office may recommend him; for the said office guarantees the honesty of its commissionaire in amounts varying from $15 to $50, besides acquainting the employer with his previous record, should he desire same; and hence the confidence of the would-be employer is at once obtained.

There are in this country to-day numerous hunters and shooters and others, whose occupation is confined to a very limited period of time yearly; all such could find lucrative employment through such an organization as "The Corps of Commissionaires,' and which must be made an outgrowth of the "National Gun Corps;" for the financial support required to organize the former, must be obtained through the latter, and thus the confidence of the latter and the support of the citizens who will aid the Gun Corps, will be obtained for the Commissionaires individually.

Hence, it is to be hoped that all owners of a shot-gun will lend their cordial support towards making a success of the above two features, with the assurance that the same will redound to the benefit of themselves and "the cause."

All parties desiring to join The National Gun Association, as contributing members—The National Gun Corps, as active members—The Corps of Commissionaires, in the capacity of the latter, are requested to communicate with the Secretary of the Association, Box 1292, Cincinnati, O.

It is proposed to start the Corps of Commissionaires by opening a sub-office for same in New York City about Sept. 1st, 1885; address communications then, to "Secretary The National Gun Association, care Von Lengerke and Detmold, 14 Murray Street, New York, City. All honorably discharged soldiers from the U. S. Army and Navy are particularly invited to join this body upon the same conditions as others

The following letter will prove especially interesting as it emanates from one most prominently identified with the founding of THE NATIONAL RIFLE ASSOCIATION :

NEW YORK, *February 5, 1885.*

DEAR SIR:—I would be glad to do anything in my power, in regard to the National Gun Association, as I think all those things have a tendency to advance the interest in and the use of arms. I do not, however, profess to be anything more than an amateur, as regards the shot gun.

I would be very glad to comply with your request to make some suggestions and hints in regard to the formation of a new Association, but do not know that anything I could say would prove valuable. The formation of the National Rifle Association has been the foundation of rifle shooting in America, and I should think the formation of a similar association would not fail to be valuable in establishing a uniform system of shooting, and providing for a central organization, which should be regarded by all local clubs as being representatives and where the subject will be looked at in the general interests of everybody. The great difficulty of an rganization of this character, is that it necessarily must be somewhat centralized and self-electing. The distances are so great that it is very hard to get those who are merely sportsmen to travel the distance that is necessary to attend a convention. With the Driving Associations and similar bodies it is different; because there large pecuniary interests are involved and men can afford to give their time to attend conventions, which Sportsmen cannot do. On the financial question you will find the institutions of life memberships to be valuable. Many who do not shoot, will be willing to pay $25.00. or so in a lump, to help the thing along, and thus supply the money which is needed. In rifle shooting, we find that the dues of annual members will go but a little way towards supplying expenses.

I should think that the Association will have a good future, as this class of shooting is more exciting and better calculated to draw the public than rifle matches.

Very truly yours,

GEO. W. WINGATE.

LIEUT. J. E BLOOM.

TRAP-SHOOTING RULES

ADOPTED BY THE NATIONAL GUN ASSOCIATION.

INDEX.

ARTICLE I.—Réferee and Judges.
    Rule 1.—Decision of Judges.
    " 2.—Decision of Referee.
    " 3.—Exclusive duties of Referee.

ARTICLE II.—The Score and Scoring.
    Rule 4.—Order of Shooting.
    " 5.—Flags for Judges.
    " 6.—Use of Second Barrel.
    " 7.—Scoring incorrect Handicap.
    " 8.—Closing of Entries.
    " 9.—Class Shooting.
    " 10.—Names Claimed.
    " 11.—Score with Ink only.

ARTICLE III.—The Traps.
    Rule 12.—Arrangement of Traps.
    " 13.—Setting of Traps.
    " 14.—Pulling of Traps.
    " 15.—Position of Puller.
    " 16.—Screens, Netting, Trench.
    " 17.—Traps for Ties.
    " 18.—Traps for Double Birds.

ARTICLE IV.—The Gun.
    Rule 19.—Position of Gun.
    " 20.—Loading of Gun.
    " 21.—Handicap of Gun.

ARTICLE V.—The Inanimate Target or Clay Pigeon.
    Rule 22.—Broken or Dead Bird.
    " 23.—Lost Birds.
    " 24.—Imperfect or "No Birds."
    " 25.—Allowing another Bird.
    " 26.—"Double Birds."

ARTICLE VI.—Rises and Ties.
    Rule 27.—The Rise
    " 28.—Ties.
    " 29.—Time of Shooting Ties.
    " 30.—Extreme Limit Tie.

ARTICLE VII.—Team Shooting.
- Rule 31.—What constitutes a Club.
- " 32.—Age of Clubs and Members.
- " 33.—Order of Shooting.
- " 34.—What constitutes a Team.
- " 55.—No division of 1st Championship Prize

ARTICLE VIII.—Purses.
- Rule 36.—Division of Purses.
- " 37.—Association Percentage.
- " 38.—Paying for Birds.
- " 39.—Guaranteed Purses.

ARTICLE IX.—Handicaps
- Rule 40.—No Handicaps for Championships.
- " 41.—Permanent Handicap.
- " 42.—Temporary Handicap.
- " 43.—New Members' Handicap.
- " 44.—Non-winners' Match Handicap.
- " 45.—Extra Match Handicap.

ARTICLE X.—Cards.
- Rule 46.—Handicap Cards.
- " 47.—Pigeon Cards.
- " 48.—Winners' Cards.

ARTICLE XI.—Prohibitions and Fines.
- Rule 49.—Non-members' Prohibition.
- " 50.—Wire Cartridges Prohibited.
- " 51.—Muzzle-loaders Prohibited
- " 52.—Fines.
- " 53.—Fines for boisterous Wrangling.
- " 54.—Bribing.

ARTICLE XII.—The Executive Committee.
- Rule 55.—Changing Sweepstakes.
- " 56.—Barring Professional Shooters.
- " 57.—Recognize no Bets.
- " 58.—Changing Rules.
- " 59.—Duties of Chief Executive Officer.

ARTICLE XIII.—*Rule 60.*—Matches per Telegraph.

ARTICLE XIV.—The Live Pigeon.
- Rule 61.—Traps, Rise, Boundary, Challenged Bird.
- " 62.—Birds on the Wing.
- " 63.—Ties.
- " 64.—Lost Bird; No Bird.
- " 65.—Gathering Birds.

Art. I.—Referee and Judges.

Rule 1. *Decision of Judges.*—Before the commencement of any match, two impartial judges shall be selected by a majority vote of the contestants, and these two shall select a referee. The judges shall, if possible, decide all questions arising during the match. They shall decide by agreeing within five minutes, or it shall be considered to be a disagreement, and thereupon the referee shall act.

Rule 2. *Decision of Referee.*—The referee shall act only in case of a disagreement of the judges, and his decision shall be absolutely final. No persons shall make any remarks calculated to influence the judges or referee while the shot is under decision.

Rule 3. *Exclusive Duties of Referee.*—The referee shall have exclusively the following duties:

A. He shall see that the traps are properly set before and kept in proper setting during the match. He shall endeavor to make the birds conform to the flight and direction indicated in Article III of these Rules.

B. He shall test any trap upon application of a shooter, at any time, by throwing a trial bird therefrom.

C. He shall select one cartridge from those of the shooter at the score, and publicly test the same for proper loading.

D. If a bird thrown, is to be declared "no bird," he shall declare it such before the shot is taken, if possible; even if so declared, it shall be scored if accepted, whether hit or missed.

E. He shall see that each shooter, before shooting, is provided with the cards specified herein, and has complied with all the rules which qualify him to shoot.

F. He shall see that no person whatever shall stand, while the shooter is at the score, within a radius of fifteen feet from the score, the puller, scorer, judges, or referee.

G. He shall see that no challenges are allowed, except made by contesting shooters.

H. He may, in his discretion, refuse to permit a shooter to continue shooting in a round, who has not come to the score within three minutes after being called thereto by the scorer.

Art. II.—The Score and Scoring.

Rule 4. *Order of Shooting.*—In individual sweepstakes or matches, shooters shall be called to the score in the order as successively entered. When the number of birds is seven singles or under, each shooter will remain at the score until he has finished same; when the number exceeds 7 singles, each shooter shall successively fire a score of 5 singles, and, when all have done likewise, will duly repeat same until the score is finished.

When the number of birds combines "so many singles" and "so many doubles," the shooters shall first finish the "singles" as per the foregoing rule, and shall then finish the "doubles" in like manner, viz., each shooter firing at 5 pairs doubles, and then retiring, etc., etc.

Rule 5. *Flags for Judges.*—Each judge shall be provided with a red flag and a white flag or guidon. They shall raise the red flag to indicate a broken or killed bird, and the white flag to indicate "lost bird"; they shall raise both flags to indicate a "no bird" or an "imperfect bird." The judges and scorer shall also promptly announce the score in a loud tone of voice.

Rule 6. *Use of Second Barrel.*—Where special matches are arranged, allowing the use of both barrels at single birds, a kill or break with the second barrel shall be scored one-half.

Rule 7. *Scoring Incorrect Handicap.*—No member is to shoot at a distance nearer than that at which he is handicapped. If he does so, the first time the shot shall be scored "no bird"; the second time it shall be scored a "lost bird"; and the third time he shall forfeit all rights in the contest, and be barred from all other contests during the same meeting, and be subject to such additional fines and penalties as the Constitution and By-Laws may provide.

Rule 8. *Closing of Entries.*—All entries shall close at the firing of the first gun. In large international or interstate tournaments, all entries for the first match each day shall be made before 6 P. M. of the day preceding the shoot, by depositing 10 per cent. of the entrance fee, which shall be forfeited to the management if the entry is not completed, before the firing of the first gun.

Rule 9. *Class Shooting.*—All sweepstakes shall be Class Shooting unless otherwise specified.

Rule 10. *Names Claimed.*—The Secretary shall keep a book in which he shall record the names of all members who desire to shoot under an assumed name, and record the name assumed by each. He shall make a charge of 50 cents, and no more, for each name recorded. No two members shall shoot under the same assumed name. The Secretary may, at the request of a member, issue the Handicap Card to him, bearing his assumed title only.

Rule 11. *Score with Ink only.*—All scoring shall be done with ink or indelible pencil. The scoring of a "lost" bird shall be indicated by a "0"; of a "dead" or "broken" bird by a "1."

ART. III.—THE TRAPS.

Rule 12. *Arrangement of Traps.*—Five traps shall be used. They shall be set level upon the ground, without any inequalities of setting in either, in an arc of a circle, five yards apart. The radius of the circle shall be 18 yards. The traps shall be numbered from No. 1, upon the left, to No. 5, upon the right, consecutively. In all traps, except No. 3, the fourth notch, or a maximum velocity equivalent thereto, shall be used, and the elevation of the projecting arm shall not exceed fifteen degrees, viz., so as to throw the pigeons from four to fifteen feet in vertical height above the level of the trap bottom. In trap No. 3, the third notch, or a velocity equivalent thereto, shall be used, with the same elevation. (See cut at end of Rules.)

Rule 13. *Setting of Traps.*—A straight line shall be drawn from the score, at eighteen yards in the rear, to trap No. 3, and extended to a point not further than seven yards in front of same. Traps Nos. 1 and 5 shall be set to throw their birds across this line, the crossing point being anywhere within the seven-yards point in front of trap 3. Trap No. 2 shall throw in a direction, left half quartering from the score; trap No. 4 shall throw in a direction, right half quartering from the score; and trap No. 3 shall throw straight-away.

If, after such setting of the traps, the birds, for any reason, take other directions, they shall be considered fair birds.

Rule 14. *Pulling of Traps.*—When the shooter calls "Pull," the trap shall be instantly sprung, or the bird may be refused. If pulled without notice, or more than one bird loosed, the shot may be refused; but, if taken, it is to be scored. If the shooter fails to shoot when the trap is properly pulled, it must be scored a lost bird.

Rule 15. *Position of Puller.*—The trap-puller shall stand from four to six feet behind the shooter, and shall use his own discretion in regard to which trap shall be sprung for each shooter, but he shall pull equally and regularly for all shooters.

Rule 16. *Screens, Netting, Trench.*—No screens or netting shall be used; "back stops" may be provided for trappers, not to exceed ten yards from the end traps, and not to exceed three feet in height.

But, where the grounds permit, a trench may be dug to shield the trapper, without obstructing the view of the traps from the shooter.

Rule 17. *Double Birds; Trap-setting.*—Doubles shall be thrown from traps Nos. 2 and 3.

Trap No. 3 shall be set at about fifteen degrees elevation; trap No. 2 at about twenty degrees elevation, in double-bird shooting; and trap No. 4, when used for shooting off ties in doubles, shall be set at about the latter elevation.

Rule 18. *Ties and Traps for Ties.*—Ties on single birds shall be thrown from traps Nos. 1, 2 and 5.

Ties on double birds from traps Nos. 3 and 4.

Art. IV.—The Gun.

Rule 19. *Position of Gun.*—The gun shall be held below the armpit, until the shooter calls "Pull;" otherwise, if challenged, the shot shall be declared a "lost" bird, whether hit or missed.

Rule 20. *Loading of Gun.*—Charge of powder unlimited; charge of shot not to exceed 1¼ oz., Dixon's standard measuse, No. 1106 "dipped" measure. Any shooter using a larger quantity of shot shall forfeit all entrance money and rights in the match, and shall be subject to further action by the management, as provided in the Constitution and By-Law's.

Rule 21. *Handicap of Gun.*—No guns larger than 10-bore shall be allowed. Guns of 12-gauge, weighing 8 pounds or under, shall be allowed two yards. Guns of smaller calibre than 12-gauge shall be shot at the same rise as the latter.

Art. V.—The Inanimate Target or Clay Pigeon.

Rule 22. *Broken Birds.*—No clay pigeons shall be retrieved to be examined for shot marks. A clay pigeon to be scored broken, must be broken so as to be plainly seen in the air; that is, a piece must be clearly and perceptibly broken from it in the air by the shot, before it touches the ground.

Rule 23. *Lost Birds.*—A. All clay pigeons, not broken in the air as above defined, and not ruled as "no birds," shall be scored lost.

B. When shooting at single clay pigeons, one barrel only shall be loaded; should more than one barrel be loaded the shot shall be scored lost.

Rule 24. *Imperfect or "No Birds."*—If a clay pigeon be broken by the trap, it shall be optional with the shooter to accept it; if he accepts, the result shall be scored.

Rule 25. *Allowing another Bird.*—The shooter shall be allowed another clay pigeon under either of the following contingencies:

A. In single-bird shooting, if two or more are sprung instead of one.

B. If the pigeon is sprung before or at any noticeable interval after the shooter calls "Pull."

C. If the pigeon does not fly 25 yards from its trap, passing over a line (imaginary), at a distance of ten yards from the traps, and 4 feet high at the latter distance. The spirit of this rule is to this effect: that the bird shall attain an elevation of not less than 4 feet within 10 yards from the trap.

D. If the shooter's gun, being properly loaded and cocked, does not go off through any cause whatever, except through the fault of the shooter.

E. If a pigeon is thrown so that to shoot in proper time, it would endanger life or property.

But if the shooter, in either of the foregoing contingencies, fires at the pigeon, he is to be deemed as accepting it, and the shot must be scored according to its result.

Rule 26. *Double Birds.*—A. In case one be a fair bird and the other an imperfect or no bird, the shooter shall shoot at a new pair; both birds must be sprung at once, otherwise they shall be "no birds."

B. If a shooter fires both barrels at one bird in succession, they shall be scored lost.

C. In double-bird shooting, in case of misfire of either barrel, through no fault of the shooter, he shall shoot at another pair.

Art. VI.—Rises and Ties.

Rule 27. *The Rise.*—The rise, in championship matches and in sweepstakes, where no handicap has been recorded, when 10-bore guns are used, shall be eighteen yards in single, and fifteen yards for double clay pigeon shooting, When ties are shot off, the rise shall be increased two yards until the limit of the handicap is reached. See handicap rules.

Rule 28. *Ties.*—Ties shall be shot at singles at three birds each and at doubles at one pair.

Ties in championship matches shall be shot at five singles (thrown from the five traps) and two doubles.

Rule 29. *Time of Shooting Ties.*—All ties shall be shot off on the same grounds, immediately after the match, if they can be concluded before sunset. If they can not, they shall be concluded on the following day, unless otherwise directed by the judges. This, however, shall not prevent the ties from dividing the prizes by agreement. Should one refuse to divide, then the tie must be shot off. Any one of the persons tieing, being absent thirty minutes after the time agreed upon to shoot them off, without permission of the judges, shall forfeit his right to shoot in the tie.

Rule 30. *Extreme Limit Tie.*—When a shooter is to shoot off a tie, who has previously thereto been handicapped to the extreme limit, he and his opponents shall shoot in the tie at the same distance they each occupied when it occurred.

Art. VII.—Team Shooting.

Rule 31. *What Constitutes a Club.*—The only club which will be recognized by the Association for the purpose of contests, is a club which has been duly organized, with the usual officers, and a *bona fide* membership of permanent standing, which maintains its organization by stated meetings and practical work. No clubs can be extemporized and admitted solely for the purpose of shooting in contests.

Rule 32. *Age of Clubs and Members.*—Clubs entering teams must be known as regularly organized gun clubs at least one month previous to the tournament; members of entered teams must be in good standing the same length of time, and be indorsed by the President and Secretary of their respective clubs. Shooters belonging to two or more clubs, must shoot with their home clubs, and can shoot with one team only.

Rule 33. *Order of Shooting.*—The teams, in team shoots, will be called to the "score" in the order designated by the Executive Committee; said order will be determined by the dates of original entry, teams being allowed to choose accordingly; the members of the team will be called to the "score" in the order designated by their respective captains, each member shooting at five single birds in succession, and then (when all teams have finished shooting at single birds) the members will, in a similar manner, finish their scores at the double birds.

Rule 34. *What Constitutes a Team.*—In team championship matches, teams of three to five must be residents of the same State, and in twin team championship matches both must be residents of the same county or parish. Any State or county can enter as many teams as they see fit. In team or club matches other than championships, there shall be no restrictions as to residence of members excepting as stated in the programme.

Rule 35. *No Division of First Championship Prize.*—In all championship matches, whether teams or individuals, there shall be no division of prizes or purses among the first scorers or winners of first championship prizes, money or badges, under penalty of expulsion from the Association.

Art. VIII.—Purses.

Rule 36. *Division of Purses*—In sweepstake matches, if the number of entries is less than twelve, the net purses shall be divided in two sums, viz.: 60% and 40%; if the number of entries is over twelve and less than forty, the net purses shall be divided into three sums, viz.: 50%, 30%, and 20%. If the number exceeds forty, the net purses shall be divided into four sums, viz.: 40%, 30%, 20% and 10%.

Rule 37. *Association Percentage.*—In all tournaments conducted by the Association, five per cent. shall be first deducted from all purses for the benefit of the Association; clubs shall deduct two per cent. in club matches, should the club so elect.

Rule 38. *Paying for Birds.*—The price of birds shall be extra, excepting in miss-and-out matches, where it shall be deducted from the entrance purse.

RULE 39. *Guaranteed Purse.*—Where a purse is guaranteed by the Association, if the entrance fees collectively exceed the guaranteed purse, all such excess shall accrue to the guarantors, viz., the Association; if less, then the Association shall supply the deficiency. Purses mentioned in the programme are not guaranteed, unless especially so stated.

ART. IX.—HANDICAPS.

RULE 40. *No Handicaps for Championships.*—In championship contests there shall be no handicap, except for guns; nor shall winners of such contests in team championships, be handicapped on account of such winning.

RULE 41. *Permanent Handicap.*—There shall be a Permanent Handicap for each shooter in all other than in championship matches. This handicap shall be made by the Executive Committee, who, immediately after each international or interstate tournament, shall classify every participant therein, and assign to him a handicap which may range from fifteen up to, but not exceed, twenty yards, for singles, and three yards less for doubles. Such handicap shall attach to such shooter thereafter (until altered) in every tournament and match in which he shall engage, when he is shooting in any association sweepstakes; and he must daily begin his shooting at this handicap.

RULE 42. *Temporary Handicap.*—In addition to the permanent handicap there shall be a temporary daily handicap, as follows: If a shooter, having already a Permanent Handicap, shall become a winner in a daily shoot, he shall be handicapped because of such winning, in accordance with the following rule: All winners or dividers of first money shall be handicapped two yards; winners (or dividers) of second money shall be handicapped one yard; maximum handicap, 22 yards. That is to say, if by the scorer's card it appears he is a winner or divider of first money, he shall be handicapped two yards, and of second money, one yard. Winners of third money are not to be handicapped for such winning. Upon presenting the scorer's card, which entitles the shooter to payment of his winnings, the executive officer shall, when paying, mark upon the shooter's handicap card the temporary handicap thus made, which shall govern for the remainder of that day. Provided, however, that in no event shall the maximum of the permanent and temporary handicaps combined exceed 22 yards for "singles," and 3 yards less for "doubles." If the shooter still continues to win at his maximum handicap, the other shooters shall step in toward the traps, the same distance that the successful shooter would otherwise have been placed back.

RULE 43. *New Members' Handicap.*—New members, whose shooting is unknown, shall be handicapped for the first time as indicated in Rules 21 and 27, though the Chief Executive Officer shall be authorized to change same, at any time during the tournament, after his present match.

RULE 44. *Non-winners' Match Handicap.*—Winners in sweepstake matches which are open only to non-winners in previous programme matches, shall not be handicapped on account of said winnings in the future programme matches of the same tournament, but said winners shall be handicapped in all extra matches, whether shot at the main five traps, or at any extra traps which may be in use on the grounds.

RULE 45. *Extra Match Handicap.*—All matches duly announced in the programme are termed "Programme Matches;" all others, "Extra Matches," whether shot at the main five traps, or at any other traps in use on the grounds. Winners in all "Extra Matches" shall be handicapped according to the above rules in all subsequent extra matches only.

ARTICLE X.—CARDS.

RULE 46. *Handicap Cards.*—The Secretary of the Association shall issue to each member a Handicap Card, which shall bear on its face the name of the shooter, the date of issue, and his permanent handicap, and blanks for temporary handicap records and payment of annual dues. The Secretary shall keep a record of all such cards issued. In the absence of the Secretary, the Chief Executive Officer of the Association on the grounds of a shoot, shall issue such card to any member who has not obtained one, and make a duplicate thereof, to be forwarded to the Secretary.

If the permanent handicap is changed by the Executive Committee, the old card shall be surrendered at the time of issuing the new one.

A permanent handicap shall not be changed during a shooting contest.

When a shooter is called to the score, he shall show his Handicap card to the scorer (who will mark the handicap on the score book), and also to the referee.

Shooters must provide themselves with Handicap Cards before going to the score.

The Chief Executive Officer shall countersign all Handicap Cards issued by the Secretary. At the beginning of a tournament shooters shall present their cards to the executive officer to be countersigned.

RULE 47. *Pigeon Cards.*—The Secretary shall provide the Chief Executive Officer with "Pigeon Cards," which, for live pigeons, shall bear the numbers from 1 to 20, inclusive, and shall be sold by the executive officer for $5.00; and which, for clay pigeons or other artificial targets, shall be numbered from 1 to 33, inclusive, and shall be sold for $1.50. The same shall bear the signature of the Secretary and the Chief Executive Officer. The scorer will punch these before the pigeons are used. All shooters must provide themselves with the respective cards before going to the score, and unused portions thereof will be redeemed at the rate at which they were issued.

RULE 48. *Winners' Cards.*—At the conclusion of each match, the scorer shall announce the winners, and shall fill out a card containing date, place, and number of the match, name of the winner, and whether 1st, 2d, or 3d, etc., number of entries, amount of entrance fee, percentage to be deducted, and sign it as scorer. The winner shall present it to the Executive Officer, who, after adding the Temporary Handicap to his record card, shall thereupon pay the amount stated, and make a record of it in his minute book.

Any complaint as to the amount stated must be made before receiving payment. These cards must subsequently be transmitted by the Executive Officer to the Secretary.

ART. XI.—PROHIBITIONS AND FINES.

RULE 49. *Prohibitions.*—None but members shall shoot in any contest, unless otherwise announced in the special rules by the Executive Committee.

RULE 50. *Wire Cartridges Prohibited.*—Wire cartridges and concentrators are, on the ground of safety, strictly prohibited; also the admixture of dust, grease, oil, or any other substance with the shot.

RULE 51. *Muzzle-loaders Prohibited.*—On the ground of safety, and for the general convenience of the shooters, muzzle-loaders are prohibited.

RULE 52. *Fines.*—A fine of one dollar, to be added to the purses, shall be rigidly exacted for any of the following acts of negligence:

A. Pointing a gun at any one under any circumstances.

B. Firing off a gun, except when the shooter has been called to shoot, and is at the score.

C. Closing a gun, with cartridge in, before arriving at the score, or pointing it towards the shooter or spectators when in the act of closing it.

D. Quitting the score without extracting a loaded cartridge unfired.

E. Having a loaded gun anywhere on the ground, except when at the score.

RULE 53. *Fines for Boisterous Wrangling.*—Should any contestant attempt to take any undue advantage of a shooter when at the score, in order to cause him to lose a bird, or should any contestant create or participate in any disturbance or loud, boisterous wrangling during a shoot, he shall be fined not less than $5, or expelled from the Association in the manner provided for in the Constitution and By-Laws.

RULE 54. *Bribery.*—Any shooter convicted of an attempt to bribe, or in any manner influence the trappers, judges, scorers, referee, or pullers, shall be barred from all further contest during the tournament, and shall be expelled from the Association.

ART. XII.—EXECUTIVE COMMITTEE.

RULE 55. *Changing Sweepstakes.*—Through the Chief Executive Officer, the Executive Committee reserve the right to add to, change, or omit any sweepstakes or matches.

RULE 56. *Barring Professional Shooters.*—They reserve the right to bar out, upon request of any two amateur shooters in the match, any publicly known professional shooter, and also any shooter who is well known to them to be ungentlemanly or disputatious.

RULE 57. *Recognize no Bets.*—They will not recognize bets, nor decide any matters arising from them. Neither shall judges or referees do so.

RULE 58. *Changing Rules.*—Rules announced to govern a tournament shall not be changed within thirty days of the date of the tournament; but while a tournament is progressing, rules may be made to govern future tournaments.

RULE 59. *Duties of Chief Executive Officer.*—All entrance moneys shall be held by the chief executive officer representing the Association on the grounds. He shall divide the purses, retaining the percentages. He shall mark with ink on the handicap card of the winners the date and the temporary handicap for the day, and shall make a record thereof in his daily minute book.

He shall take charge of the score books every night during a tournament.

He shall have authority to employ such subordinates as he may require.

He shall countersign the handicap cards. He shall have authority to change the permanent handicap cards of unknown members.

He shall sell the "Pigeon Cards" and redeem any unused parts thereof.

ART. XIII.—MATCHES PER TELEGRAPH.

RULE 60. Teams or individuals may arrange matches, or the Association may arrange same, to be shot by each at their own respective localities, without coming together, upon complying with the following conditions, viz.:

The entrance fee shall be sent by mail to the Secretary of the Association, to reach him before the shooting begins. If the entrance fee is not sent by mail, it may be sent by telegraph one hour before the shooting begins. Any person not a member, who desires to enter, may send by mail or telegraph, one hour before the shooting begins, an initiation or member's fee of $5.00, and the entrance fee beside.

All the rules heretofore stated shall apply equally to such matches. Members shall shoot at their permanent handicaps. Those who have no handicap record, shall shoot at the usual distance, 18 yards, etc. The result of each score must be telegraphed as the same is made, to the Secretary of the Association. The scores must also be mailed to him the same day, and their accuracy certified to by the President and Secretary of the local club, or by two disinterested and responsible witnesses who saw the shooting, and who are members of the Association.

Ties shall be shot off, under these rules, upon the twentieth weekday thereafter.

The Executive Committee of the Association will duly announce the result, and decide upon any controverted points. The committee shall have full power to make inquiry as to the accuracy of the scores as reported, and to award the money according as the facts may appear.

ART. XIV.—THE LIVE PIGEON.

The following rules (in addition to and modification of the preceding rules), apply to live pigeon matches only :

RULE 61. *The Traps, Rise, Boundary, Challenged Bird.*—All live birds shall be shot from ground traps, which shall be set five yards apart. Rise 25 yards. Use of one barrel only. Boundary unlimited. In case of challenged bird, the shooter allowed three minutes to gather it.

RULE 62. *Birds on the Wing.*—In double-bird shooting, the birds shall be on the wing when shot at. A bird shot on the ground shall be scored lost. Double birds to be shot at 21 yards rise, boundary unlimited; five minutes allowed to gather birds if challenged.

RULE 63. *Ties.*—On single birds, 25 yards rise; doubles, at 21 yards rise.

RULE 64. *Lost Birds; No Bird.*—If a bird is shot at, by any person other than the shooter at the score, the referee shall decide whether it shall be scored lost, or whether he will allow another bird. When traps are sprung, should a bird refuse to fly after a reasonable time, the shooter may call "no bird."

RULE 65. *Gathering Birds.*—It shall be optional with the shooter to gather his own birds or appoint a person to do so for him. In all cases the bird must be gathered by hand, without any forcible means, within three minutes from the time it alights, or it shall be scored a lost bird. All live birds must show shot marks if challenged.

Arrangement of Traps.

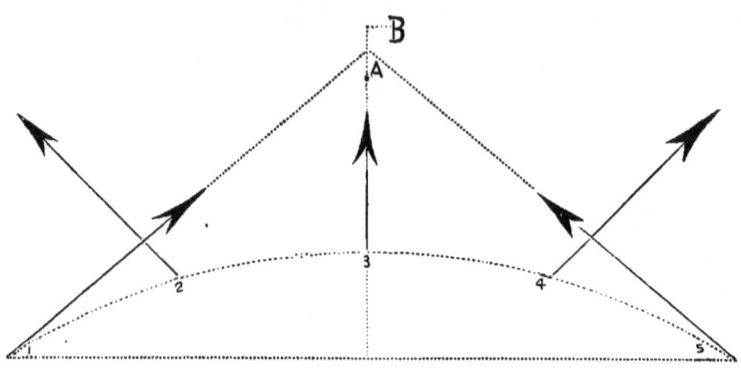

Scale 1 inch—5 yards.

Nos. 1, 2, 3, 4 and 5 indicate position of traps, located 5 yards apart on the arc of a circle whose radius is 18 yards. The full arrow-pointed lines indicate the directions towards which the birds should fly, and towards which the projecting arms of the trap should point before "trapping"; the 'score" is on the extension of line B 3; "B" is the 7 yard point beyond trap "3", within which the lines of flight from traps Nos. "1" and "5" should cross the line B 3.

GUN CLUBS.

[*Extract from Turf, Field and Farm, Feb.* 27, 1885.]

A man who does not belong, or has never belonged to a gun club, has missed much of the pleasure of club matches, as well as the enjoyment members have among themselves in suppers and meetings.

The first requisite for a gun club, is to have enough members of importance in a community to join, to have some respect paid to it as an organization. There are districts and counties in every State, where there are no gun clubs, but any number of shooters, which would be much better if an organization was effected for trap shooting and game protective purposes.

Trap shooting contests are necessary to bring together shooters, where single meetings for game protection purposes would not collect as many. A move in the right direction is now being made, to combine these into a National Gun Association, a stock company, and organized under the laws of Kentucky.

This has been tried before, and at present seems likely to be successful under a vigorous management.

HOW TO FORM A GUN CLUB.

In forming a gun club, the first thing to do is to get a number of shooters to meet in some convenient room, and any one who possesses a good knowledge of parliamentary law can act as temporary chairman by acclamation. He then states the object of the meeting. A motion is made that an organization be effected, stating the name of the association; another motion follows that a committe of three be appointed to draft a constitution and by-laws, to be reported at the next meeting. A good parliamentarian is then elected president, who has a first-class knowledge of all that appertains to shooting. A vice-president follows of nearly equal ability. A careful and accurate secretary is necessary to take the minutes, and a good collector and accountant for treasurer. The best trap-shot is usually elected captain of the team, and three or five good workers as the board of directors, or executive committee.

In gun clubs, the post of captain of the team is a position that requires something more than being a first-class shot, as I know from experience. He must coach his men in a match in order to keep up their nerve, and selecting shooters after seeing them practice continually, to take those that can always be depended on making a certain tolerably good score, instead of those that make a poor score one day, and a first-class one the next. The captain of a club team must know every rule perfectly, to see that other clubs do not take an unfair advantage in shooting, by superior knowledge of all the little points that can be broken, that referees can be bulldozed into deciding favorably, or else do not know when appealed to.

A time for the next meeting is appointed, and a place looked for, to have shooting matches afterward, by the Board of Directors. With the adoption of the constitution, the organization is complete.

If the club has well-attended matches, numerous meetings where some real business is done in regard to game and its protection or restocking depleted districts, some good suppers to draw out the members, and a team of five or ten that can average over eighty per cent. of clay pigeons shot at, nothing more can be asked for.

INTER-COLLEGIATE CONTESTS.

An intercollegiate association of trap shooters has been talked of at various times, but has never been formed. To have any sort of interest to the public, there should be a trophy emblematic of the championship, and an inter-collegiate association of clubs should be formed, to meet annually and revise rules for shooting. Doing things up as systematically as this does not seem likely, unless one college club will start the affair by some energetic move. Club members in college generally do not shoot as much at the traps as they do in the field, merely because there is no stimulus in the hope of prospective intercollegiate matches.

Shooting is a sport that has but recently been taken up at colleges, and the fact that some prizes have been taken at Walnut Hill range by Harvard men, shows that college gun clubs and shooters will amount to something yet. Yale used to have an excellent rifle team, just as Harvard has some good shots now, but trap shooting at clay pigeons seems to be making the most advance, and rifle shooting is thought of only as being a slower and not as exciting form of sport.

In a California college and at the Univerity of Michigan, clay pigeon shooting has been practiced, and in the colleges of the East, scarcely one has done without having an organized gun club, no matter whether they ever went shooting or not. Bowdoin, Williams, Cornell, Harvard, Princeton, Yale and Pennsylvania, as well as one or two others, all have had organizations composed of the sportsmen among the students.

The University of Pennsylvania was lately the most flourishing, having teams of ten men in each of the four classes, and a first-class college team of ten, every man of whom had records of clean scores; this club challenged Cornell and Harvard for the college championship, but both of the clubs evaded the challenge, and could not be got to the traps, so the U. P. claimed the championship, and still hold it until beaten.

CLUB HOUSES.

Gun clubs that have a club-house at the sea shore, and go there to shoot snipe, ducks and geese when there are flights on, are called Bay Clubs. On the Jersey coast there are a great many of these, composed generally of Philadelphians and New Yorkers, who regard this State as their natural shooting ground.

One of the best ways of enjoying a short shooting trip after wild fowl, is to belong to or be a guest of a Bay Club. It is a jovial crowd; a stag party composed of men that generally know how to have a good time when they get together. Many live like aborigines, subsisting by hunting and fishing, while all things in the way of property are in common. Some differ, though, in having elegant club houses, fitted up and upholstered in the finest style, with all manner of boats and hired men attached, to take members and invited friends out for the day. A French cook, with a big salary, probably cooks the meals, and there is no difference, as far as style goes, from the City Club House. The majority are not like this, or on such an elaborate plan, and those who belong have no house, but come down in a body and tent on the beach, live all the time in a cabin-yacht, or else stay at a hotel near some favorite spot, in a body, and generally have the run of the place. This latter way is the most indulged in, probably.

Trap shooting is practiced with them considerably, and many inter-club matches are shot. Glass-ball shooting is not done one-quarter as much as it was; there are newer and better substitutes for the live bird. For a while it was practiced assiduously; then came a reaction; the crystal spheres projected from a catapult called a trap (a misnomer, by the way) did not give shots exactly like the bird in rising from the field. The glass ball is shot at almost exclusively at a certain point in its flight, just where it begins to fall, usually. Now, to wait in shooting until the object begins to fall, and then fire after ascertaining its direction, is not like grouse, woodcock or quail shooting. Even rotary traps did not improve this, nor yet five set like pigeon ground-traps. Smoke balls, clay percussion balls, composition, soluble and puff balls, all failed to give complete satisfaction; birds, when flying away from the shooter, present a crescent-shaped object when the wings are lowered in flight, and when raised, a double conical appearance. The glass ball was round, and when objects [the Ligowsky clay pigeon (Ed.)] were introduced that went skimming away a long distance, on which both barrels of a gun could be fired, and which was not unlike a bird in its flight (except that the object began its speed at the highest rate, and slowly and gradually relaxed, the opposite with a pigeon) then these superseded the glass ball.

SUGGESTIONS AS TO MATCHES.

Regular matches at seven or less pigeons, clay pigeons or glass balls per man, is often no proof of the best shot being the winner. The best shot of the lot may have one hard bird close to the ground; he may miss it clean, may hit and not break it; the referee may think it broke on the ground, instead of hit by shot, or he may have his gun too high when he calls "pull," may have overloads of shot in the shell, may not load when he comes to the score, or load before doing so; anyway, it will be a cipher on his score, and lose him first place in the match. It takes at least twenty or twenty-five shots per man at clay pigeons to tell who can shoot the finest, and more than that at live birds, because so many drop out of bounds, and lose a match in this way occasionally.

Shooting clay saucers has developed surprisingly among shooters during the last couple of years. An attachable arm to traps is now made to throw them when the pasteboard tail has come off, and is a good addition. If this could be made to throw as far as with the tail on, it would be adopted in preference, not only on account of being more convenient, but clays would be cheaper. The flight depends very much on the angle at which the trap is set, and which direction the wind blows. A clay pigeon going, four feet from the ground, directly to the right or left, is the hardest kind a shooter can get, if the trap is set at the fourth notch. The clays require quick handling of the gun, and are not like glass balls thrown from an old Bogardus trap, shot at only in a certain part of their flight. Anybody at a stationary trap can get the level, and lift up and fire at the ball just when it begins to fall in the flight. An ordinary shot may be a crack wing shot at this, if he gets the level of the rise of the crystal sphere. A clay pigeon is different, and the traps as well; in it the best wing shot always wins, if he shoots up to his regular form.

"Trap and handle" matches are the hardest kind to score under. Two men shoot against each other; one takes a turn at shooting five shots, say, while the other fills the traps and handles the cords when pulling in such a way as to puzzle the shooter as much as possible, and then he takes his turn at the strings when the other is ready to shoot. With pigeons one party selects the hardest to hit and the fastest flyers he can get for the other, and often a match is won of this class by a shooter being "out-birded." Clay pigeons can be set to give eccentric flights, if one takes a morning to study the way of arranging the tail in the grip of the lever.

In these matches every advantage possible is taken of the rules by both parties, and until the whole match is finished it may be either of the shooters, because one may attempt to take unfair advantage of the other, and the contestant may at the close of the match make a written protest to referee, claiming the match, whether his score is the best or not. Rules generally have this embodied in them.

One of the things done occasionally is kicking at rules agreed on beforehand, but which, when the shooter tries to break them and the penalty is enforced, immediately raises a row in a very ungentlemanly manner, and loses control of his temper. Men who will not stick to rules agreed upon beforehand, are debarred from stakes and match by a written protest; also if they will not finish the score when the other is ahead, or wait more than five minutes when called to the score.

It is the only protection one can have when competitors will not stand at the scratch while they shoot, when they shoot with gun above the elbow; if the rules forbid this when calling "pull," if they load or have the gun loaded away from the scratch before shooting, thus recklessly endangering the life of the trap-setter by a premature discharge; if they try all the time to claim on others birds as missed, when evidently hit; when they fix the cord around the trap to balk the shooter when ready to fire, and make him lose confidence in the trap going off at all, or refuse to pay the stakes when fairly one, according to rules agreed upon beforehand. Men of this stamp are worse than any professional, and I would suggest having their names blacklisted to keep any one from shooting in their company.

THE NATIONAL GUN ASSOCIATION.

The secretary of the "National Gun Association" should be furnished with a list of such men by presidents of clubs to which such have unfortunately belonged, and publish them, so that they can be barred from participating in any matches held by the association or clubs belonging to it.

Every man that belongs to a gun club should have the members of it join the National Gun Association, and every individual trap shooter, whether he belongs to a club or not, should help such a worthy object, as its constitution shows it to be, along by financial aid.

CAMDEM, N. J., FEB. 22, 1885.

Comments of Prominent Sportsmen.

LOUISVILLE, KY., Dec. 31, 1884.
MR. J. E. BLOOM, ESQ., CINCINNATI, OHIO.
DEAR SIR:
    Yours of yesterday received and contents carefully noted, and will say your plans have my approval, and I think the move will materialize into something good. If I can get to New Orleans I will gladly give my aid to the move; it may be changed in some particulars after a full discussion by all present; but there is one thing certain (that all will admit), that we need a set of national rules for all kinds of shooting, to be known as the *American Rules.*

    Yours Truly,
        J. M. BARBOUR,
          PRES'T LOUISVILLE SPORTSMAN'S ASS'N.

SAVANNAH, GA., January 9, 1885.
J. E. BLOOM, ESQ. CINCINNATI.
DEAR SIR:
    I heartily approve of your plan and say, you can use my name. I hope to visit New Orleans next month and hope to bring a team with me. I believe we will all join the association.

    Yours Truly,
        WM. G. COOPER,
          President of Chatham Gun Club.

MICHIGAN SPORTSMEN'S ASSOCIATION
FOR THE PROTECTION OF FISH, GAME AND BIRDS.

GRAND RAPIDS, MICH., Jan. 12, 1885.
J. E. BLOOM, *et al.* DEAR SIR:
    Your circular containing a prospectus of the National Gun Association is received, and in general meets with my approval. Although I do very little trap-shooting, yet the fact stares us in the face, that we will be obliged to relinquish sport and recreation with the gun soon, or partake of it before the traps. In fact, with a great many this is practically true now. Hence, the desirability of a court of last resort in all matters pertaining to this species of out-door enjoyment. But allow me to suggest, would it not be well to substitute American for "National" and include Canada?

* * * * * * * * *

    Yours Truly,   E. S. HOLMES,
          Pres't Mich. Sportsmen's Ass'n

SPRINGFIELD, O., January 8, 1885.
MR. J. E. BLOOM, Esq.
DEAR SIR AND FRIEND:
Your circular letter at hand, and contents carefully noted. It meets my full approval; I am quite enthusiastic in seeing such a scheme in vogue. Last year I formed what we called our "Central Ohio Shooting Association" and we held monthly shoots at Kenton, Bellefontaine, Greenville, Urbana and Springfield; one month at Kenton, next at Bellefontaine, next at Greenville &c., and we always had good attendance. We charged three dollars admission and at any shoot we allowed a shooter the privilege of becoming a member by payment in advance of action of association.

We also charged 5cts. each for birds (clay) and 20cts. each for birds (live). We always made a nice little profit from each tournament.

The original twenty in the scheme have seen their stock double, that is to say our $2 are worth $4, and we are only in our first year. We charge $1 yearly dues, always payable in advance and before a shooter is allowed any privileges in the tournament.

Go on with your scheme it will secure the support of our boys. Yours very truly,
L. E. RUSSELL, M. D.,
Pres't Central Ohio Sportsmen's Ass'n.

DU QUOIN, ILL., January 11, 1885.
J. E. BLOOM,
CINCINNATI, O.
DEAR SIR:
Yours in relation to forming a "National Shooters Association," to hand, and in reply to it would say, that while I have no interest in such an association except as an individual sportsman and my love for trap and field shooting, I am perfectly willing that my name be used as one of the willing workers, if it will add any strength to the cause.

It is quite evident to my mind that a National Association, well officered and properly managed, with sensible rules to govern, would be a great benefit to the trap-shooters of this country.

A circuit of tournaments would be something that would afford pleasure for all sportsmen, while a set of National Rules for all kinds of trap shooting are very much needed.

Yours Truly,
C. P. RICHARDS,
Sec'y Southern Ills. Sportsmen's Ass'n.

THE NATIONAL GUN ASSOCIATION. 49

NEW YORK, N. Y., January 16, 1885.
MR. J. E. BLOOM.
MY DEAR SIR:—Your letters and circulars about a National Association came to hand. As you may know I am heart and soul in the movement and will do whatever I can; you can put me down for a life-member share and as one of the workers.   Very Truly Yours,
JUSTUS VON LENGERKE.

LEADVILLE, COL., January 12, 1895.
J. E. BLOOM, ESQ.
DEAR SIR:—Your circular at hand and meets my ideas exactly. You can put me down for five shares, ($25.00) twenty-five dollars.
Yours Truly,
GEO. B. DOUGAN.

ELIZABETH, N. J., January 12, 1885.
J. E. BLOOM, ESQ.
DEAR SIR:—I am in receipt of circular prospectus of National Gun Association. I think it a good thing, and have often wondered why such an association has not been started before. If I understand it rightly, any one belonging to a regular organized Gun Club may invest in shares from five (5) dollars upward, by paying on five dollar shares one dollar per month, and larger shares 10 per cent per month. I want to thoroughly understand it, as I intend to present this circular at the next Club meeting for the consideration of the members. Another thing I want to ask: Can one after having taken, say a five dollar share. add as many shares afterward to come up to the limit.   WM. W. PARKER,
Treasurer Elizabeth Gun Club.

ANSWER:—Your understanding is correct as to the monthly subscription payment; those taking one share pay $1.00 per month, though the first payment will not be more than 50 cts. (10 per cent.); those taking more than one share pay 10 per cent. per month on the total subscription. Any person taking one share and desiring to add thereto subsequently, can do so, paying 10 per cent. monthly on the total amount then subscribed, provided of course, there are any shares remaining for subscription. The Association will be organized with a capital stock depending on the views of the sportsmen assembling at New Orleans; it may be $1,000, $2,500 or $5,000—probably the latter amount. When the same is once all subscribed, of course no more can be obtained by anyone from the association; they can then only be obtained by purchasing from those who have already subscribed, which fact will in my estimation always give the stock a good market value independent of the dividend-paying qualities.

There is no limit to the number of shares for which anyone may now subscribe, though it would be best, if the project could be carried out limiting the subscription to five shares.   Respectfully,
J. E. BLOOM.

PHILADELPHIA, PA., January 16, 1884.
MR. J. E. BLOOM,
DEAR SIR:—Your circular in regard to the National Gun Association to hand. Your plan seemed a little complicated at first, but, after reflection, conceded it a wise conclusion. You may add me as a "worker," and shall in all probability subscribe to some stock.   Yours truly,
C. A. BRAGG,
Manager Globe Shot Co.

CINCINNATI, O., January 7, 1885.

J. E. BLOOM, ESQ.
MY DEAR SIR:—Yours received and contents noted. I fully agree with you and think it is a long felt want. You may add my name to your list and rest assured that I will give you my support and do all in my power to make it a success.
Yours Truly,
AL. BANDLE,
Pres't Cin'ti Gun Club.

EXETER, January 17, 1885.
MR. J. E. BLOOM,
MY DEAR SIR:—Your circular announcing the prospectus of the National Gun Association duly received. I think the suggestions and ideas advanced are in the right direction and to the point, and I shall do all in my power to further the project. Our small club will be represented by a team of three men at least, and I trust the tourney at New Orleans may be as successful as the first one held last year at Chicago.
Fraternally Yours,
DR. C. H. GERRISH,
Pres't New England Trap Shooters Association.

WASHINGTON, D. C., January 17, 1885.
MR. J. E. BLOOM.
DEAR SIR:—You can add my name to the list as one of the workers for getting up a Trap Shooters Association; will do all I can to help it to prosper.
Yours Truly.
WM. WAGNER.

UNIONTOWN, KY., January 17, 1885.
MR. J. E. BLOOM,
DEAR SIR:—I heartily indorse your plan of the National Gun Association; you can put me down as an "active worker." That is, you have my approval and influence.
I am Secretary and Treasurer of the "Highland Gun Club" of this place, will present your plan before the club at our next meeting.
I suggest that something be added to this association to require each member to see that the game law is fully enforced; and stringent laws made to protect game where old laws are deficient
Respectfully,
R. W. CRABB.

HENRIETTA, CLAY CO., TEX., January 13, 1885.
DEAR SIR:—Your circular at hand. In regard to the National Gun Association, you can put me down for one share; and if ever I am in a place to do trap-shooting, then I shall be a member.
Just now my home abounds with game, and I can only encourage my friends, who are not so fortunate with a little assistance, and I hope every sportsman who handles a gun will do the same. You will please to sign for me in New Orleans, as I am afraid I shall be unable to attend, and notify me where the ballance of the five dollars is to be paid; Enclosed find 50 cents in postage stamps.
Yours Very Truly,
B. R. BUFFHAM.
"ALMO."

FLEMINGTON, N. J., January 1-12, 1885.

MR. J. E. BLOOM.

SIR:—I see in the *Turf, Field and Farm* you give two plans for forming a National Association at the shooting tournament at New Orleans, and I would say that the first is the best that I have yet seen, but the second is a good one; and I would suggest that whatever plan is adopted, it will hold four Inter-State Tournaments each year, and one International. I will not be at the Tournament, but I will agree with any plan adopted and I herewith enclose ten (10) per cent of amount for one share for forming the second plan; and you can put my name down as a member of said Association whichever way it is formed, and would request that you keep me posted as to the matter. I would also suggest that one Director be elected in each State represented, and that the next Tournament be held at Philadelphia, Pa.

Yours Truly,
GEO. E. READING.

BOSTON, MASS., January 19, 1885.

MT. J. E. BLOOM,

DEAR SIR:—Your favor accompanying prospectus of the "National Gun Association" duly to hand. As you are doubtless well aware, I do not consider myself a thorough shotgun man, my specialty heretofore having been the rifle. Yet I confess to a sufficient liking for the shot gun, to cause me to devote considerable time, effort and money in my endeavors to promote the use of it in our own (The Massachusetts Rifle) Association, and in this section of the country; partially because of the personal enjoyment that I derive from the use of the gun, and more largely from the good fellowship that I enjoy thereby. * * I am heartily in sympathy with the enterprise and shall be pleased to see its success assured. There are principles involved in the prospectus that I heartily and fully endorse, and with the view to securing harmony among sportsmen, hope for the formation and adoption of a code of shooting rules, that will become standard rules throughout the country. Any assistance I can render to further the success of efforts in this direction, will be cheerfully rendered. Hastily and Truly Yours,

JAS. N. FRYE.

EVANSVILLE, IND., January 8, 1885.

DEAR SIRS:—It gives me pleasure to say "add my name to the workers." I think your idea a good one, and will do all I can to further it. It is what we need--not only for sport, but for ume protection. Yours,

F. M. GILBERT,
Game Warden, 1st Dist. Ind.

PITTSBURG, January 20, 1885.

J. E. BLOOM, ESQ.

DEAR SIR.—I have carefully read your prospectus, and for its success I sincerely hope. The organization of a National Association that shall have sufficient influence to establish a code of rules for Pigeon, Ball and Clay Pigeon Shooting will be a stupendous work. * * * I would recommend an Illinois charter, and Chicago as the place to hold the first stock-holders meeting. I speak of Chicago because your call is for a National Association, and there are but two national cities in the United States, viz.: New York and Chicago; in shooting matters the latter city is the best. You can as well have 5,000 members as 1,000, if the scheme is started on a large scale.

* * * * * * * * *

Very Truly, J. PALMER O'NEIL.

THE NATIONAL GUN ASSOCIATION.

FALMOUTH, MASS., January 19, 1885.

J. E. BLOOM, ESQ.

DEAR SIR:—The prospectus of yourself and associates came to hand, and I have for some time watched the growing interest in such an association. It is imperative to a wide and general interest in trap shooting that there should be some standard code of rules, equitable to, and recognized by all, not only to guide trap shooters who spare no money to obtain the best gun for that specific purpose; but those who indulge in the sport only as a diversion, using guns of weights and bores best adapted to their individual preferences in the field. These, when brought into competition, as they are in country clubs, with the heavy and especially adopted pigeon guns, soon lose interest in the rotating platters from a feeling of being handicapped. The move has my sincere wish for its success and my furtherance can only be limited by means and ability.

Very respectfully yours,

F. J. C. SWIFT.

CAMDEN, N. J., January 18, 1885.

DEAR SIR:—I believe the University of Pennsylvania gun club has no representation on the Comm. at present, and if you wish to add my name as an ex-president of it and captain of its team when it claimed the intercollegiate championship, will be pleased to do anything I can for you. Hope the National Trap Shooters Association will be a grand success and will try to get to New Orleans, if possible, as well as subscribe to its stock when subscription books are open.

Yours, etc.,

CLARENCE W. TAYLOR.

FLATBUSH, N. Y., January 17, 1885.

J. E. BLOOM, ESQ.

MY DEAR SIR:—I am heartily in sympathy with you and your co-workers in this movement. Now while on the financial part, there is one trait strong and predominant in man, and that is "while it is blessed to give, it is likewise to receive;" and if you can show the public any benefit o be derived from joining and supporting such an association, they will undoubtedly give aid readily as well as support. Now why not incorporate in this, a "Mutual Benefit to Sportsmen," viz: Make it on the principle of Locomotive Engine Brotherhood or any of those societies. Say for instance, a sportsman died; let every member be taxed $1.00, and the same forwarded to his family or relatives. Or if any accident happen to sportsman while traveling or shooting away from home, that all members be taxed $1.00 a piece, and the said amount appropriated as far as necessary to take care of him and return him home, etc. You will from these hurried remarks understand my meaning. * * * * * * *

Believe me, yours most truly,

WASHINGTON A. COSTER.

J. E. BLOOM, ESQ.:

The prospectus of the National Gun Association has this day been received; many thanks. You can put me down for one share, and also count on my giving any assistance in my power to further so commendable an enterprise. I only hope you may succeed in getting every thing in running order. ❋ ❋ ❋ ❋ ❋ ❋ ❋ ❋ ❋ ❋

Very Sincerely Yours, ARTHUR W. DU BRAY.

A NATIONAL SHOOTING ASSOCIATION.

[Editorial Forest and Stream, Jan. 15, '85.]

Another effort has started in the Southwest toward the formation of an association which shall embrace all the trap-shooters of the country The main idea is a good one, but is not new, and the practical difficulty lies in the preparation of such a schedule of work, such a plan of organization, as shall not strangle the body by too much law, nor allow it to drift away into nothingness through a too flimsy constitution and working code of laws.

Those who love the exhilarating and manly sport of trap-shooting ought to give a hearty support to any such effort as this last, showing as it does an earnest desire to reach the objects aimed at. There is no doubt that such an organization would lead to a largely increassd popular appreciation of this special line of sport, and not only at the score, but among the ranks of spectators, large accessions to the present showing would be had.

The plan for the new organization is sufficiently outlined in the circular issued by its suggestors to be open for popular discussion, and this we invite through our columns. Many of our readers have practical general acquaintance with the growth and failure of similar efforts in the past, and can contribute of their experience in the way of warnings against the particularly dangerous snags liable to be met. It is certain that the body should be of the most democratic type, with the minimum of dictation from managers, and the entire absence of anything like a ring. Those who support it must manage it, which means that the control must be in the hands of the shooters, and to keep it there as little as possible of routine work should be put upon those whose first and final aim is to have a good time before the trap.

Large attention should be given to the encouragement of local clubs and the development of local pride in the outcome of the matches. A big pot of money in the way of tempting individual prizes will bring a big crowd of shooters, each expert in all the little tricks and dodges which will help him to get into possession of the purse before him; but such a company soon shoots itself out, unless a carefully devised scheme of handicap be fixed. On the other hand, prizes for the best display of skill from this or that locality will often bring out a fine class of shooters, provoke an interest in people and press over the matches, and place the competitions on a more enduring basis than possible by any other plan. It will bring an entirely different set of men to the front, and a very desirable set, too, and the two different classes of matches might readily be combined with a very successful meeting. It is certainly true that a rivalry must be excited, and the best and healthiest is that which springs from some other motive than a sole wish to get possession of the stakes. It is, of course, absurd to think for a moment that such a national body can be run on a capital of glory only; there must be cash prizes, and liberal ones, too, and there would be, we think, no trouble in raising them, but the effort should not begin and end there. Som men think they are best paid when they hear the jingle of coin in their pockets, others are far better paid in the satisfaction of carrying off a championship against a field of worthy competitors.

Such a national organization may do good in fixing upon a set of rules broad enough to take in all varieties of matches, and exact enough to meet every possible complication which may arise. The experience has already been had, all that the association needs to do is to gather up hints from all quarters, take all the existing sets of rules and codify them into a working system, short, plain and just. At present there is a continuous wrangle over every possible interpretation of the existing shooting regulations, and there is no central board whose authority would be recognized, to whom the disputed questions may be sent for adjudication. The sporting press does something in this line, but it would be as well done and better by a board springing from and constituted by the sportsmen themslves.

General Beauregard,

On the proposed "National Gun Corps."

Dear Sir:

Your favor of the 7th inst. has been received. I can but approve the above amendment (Article XVI) to the Constitution of "The National Gun Association." Such an organization must necessarily increase the "esprit de corps" and usefulness of the Association. I am,

Yours very truly,

G. T. BEAUREGARD,

Adjt. Gen'l of La.

New Orleans, March 12, 1885.

CHICAGO, ILL., *February 10, 1885.*

J. E. BLOOM, ESQ.
New Orleans. La.

DEAR SIR:—It was my intention to have participated in the formation of your contemplated organization this week; but owing to sickness in my family, am compelled to forego that pleasure. However I would call your attention to Rule 6, on Guns and Rise, of your Stark-Ligowsky Rules, which reads as follows: Rise for 12 bore, 18 yards single; 15 yards on doubles; the 10 bore shall be handicapped two yards, while those of lesser gauge shall go in one yard for every size less than 12 bore.

I would suggest that the rule be changed to read as follows: "Rise for 12 bore gun *under 8 lbs. in weight*, singles 18 yards, doubles 15 yards. The 10 bore shall be handicapped two yards; while those of a lesser gauge than 12, shall go in *one-half yard*, for each gauge, providing said gun weighs less than 8lb."

As the rule now is, a man can use a 10 lb., 16 bore gun using 5 drs. powder and 1¼ oz. shot and at single birds can stand at 14 yards and at double 11 yards, while the shooter whose misfortune it is to be the owner of an 8½ lb., 10 bore, must stand back to 18 and 20 yards respectively. It is useless to handicap guns and not limit the weight; as we shoot from 5 traps, adopt the English handicap with the exception above noted. Hoping that you will organize a National Association, and that it will be a grand success,

I remain, yours truly,

R. B. ORGAN.
President, Chicago Shooting Club.

OGDEN CITY, UTAH.

J. E. BLOOM, ESQ.

DEAR SIR:—Enclosed, please find postal note. Please add to your list National Gun Asssociation members as follows:

W. D. Howe, Ogden, Utah Ty., two shares.
A. C. Smith, Prest. Ogden Shooting Club, one share.
Dr. H. H. Hurlbut, Secy. Ogden Shooting Club, one share.
Henry G. Doon. C. P. Ry. Ogden, two shares.

You can depend upon me sending you names for twenty shares more. I think our Clubs will join in a body, which will make some 70 names more. Please send me circulars to distribute.

Yours truly,

W. D. HOWE.

PHILADELPHIA, *February 19, 1885.*

J. E. BLOOM, ESQ.
Treas. Nat. Gun Ass'n.

DEAR SIR.—You will please find enclosed 50 cents, 10 per cent. of membership fee of the above association. Our trap shooters here are anxious to see your efforts a success.

Very respectfully yours,

THOMAS P. GREGER.
Vice Prest. Central State C. P. League.

BRADFORD, MASS., *February 11, 1885.*

MR. J. E. BLOOM.

Having seen an account of the attempt to get up a National Association, and thinking it would be a good thing, and being willing to help it along, I enclose postal note for 50 cents (fifty cents) for 10 per cent. subscription to one share of their capital stock. Although I am not a member of an organized gun club, I am still a great lover of the gun. Hoping that success will attend your efforts,

Yours truly,

CHARLES A. KIMBALL.

WOODLAND, CAL., *February 4, 1885.*

MR. J. E. BLOOM,
  Cincinnati, Ohio.

DEAR SIR:—I have just read your communication in my *American Field* in regard to organizing a National Association for the purpose of keeping up the interest in tournaments, &c. I enclose a dollar bill for two shares. In haste.

G. W. WATSON.
Jacobs Hall, Saramento, Cal.

WASECA, MINN., *February 8, 1885.*

DEAR SIR:—As I cannot be with you during Tournament, I enclose 50 cents in part payment of one share of Sportsmen's Association. I think the idea is excellent, and shall do all in my power to aid in its success.

Respectfully,

W. H. SKINNER.

PROVIDENCE, R. I., *February 7, 1885.*

Inclosed you will find fifty (50) cents, as ten (10) per cent. of one (1) share in the National Association.

The Club, of which I am a member, will probably join in a body (Narragansett) but I prefer to join at once and not take the chances.

Yours truly,

H. L. PALMER.

STONY POINT, N. Y., *January 17, 1885.*

Having heard of your proposed National Association through the columns of the *Forest and Stream*, and feeling deeply interested in the success of the movement, I should like to become a subscriber; I am just now engaged in forming a club of pigeon shooters in this town and shall try and have some of the members also subscribe. Please put me down for five shares.

Truly, your obedient servant,

FRED'K. TOMKINS.

ORWELL, VT., *January 20, 1885.*

Have just read the article in *Forest and Stream*, in regard to organizing a "National Association." There can be no doubt of its success. Be so kind as to book me for 5 Shares ($25.00); also, Dr. Vincent, Montpelier, Vt., for 5 shares.

Respectfully,

WILL. L. PIKE.

CLAY PIGEON AND WING SHOOTING.

By CAPT. GWYNNE PRICE, of St. Louis, Mo.

[Extract, by permission, from his book (copyrighted) with the above title.]

The first and principal object of Trap-Shooting should be the attainment of the nearest approach to perfection in the enjoyable and healthful recreation of Field shooting on the Wing.

No doubt, the practice obtained from the flight of the live pigeon, when flushed in a natural manner from a ground trap, is the best, but the difficulty in getting pigeons, *whether wild or tame*, in good condition, as well as the high price now paid for them, renders it a necessity that artificial means should be resorted to.

An inanimate object, propelled by mechanical means, is much cheaper, and naturally suggests itself as the *only* resource obtainable; but until very recently no invention has been made of sufficient utility to answer the purpose properly.

Every game bird is found upon the ground, and on being moved, makes an *upward* or *rising* flight, presenting, consequently, the most difficult of all shots, particularly so if slightly quartering. It is therefore a necessity, in order to become proficient as a wing shot, that a style of motion the *nearest approaching* to the ordinary flight of a bird, should always be used in practice.

Pigeons jerked from a plunged trap are generally shot at when falling, and the same may be said of glass balls thrown from *most* traps, such motion is therefore *diametrically opposed* to field shooting. Instead of such practice being beneficial in producing good field shots, it is exactly the reverse, for at game nearly every shot is a rising one.

Clay pigeon shooting, when the traps are set to throw the birds in every direction of quartering and straight-away slightly rising shots, is the only invention to the present time combining every element necessary to make fine game shots; and where the traps are set *according to instructions* and properly handled, will produce every style of shooting in imitation of the bird itself, of which it is the best possible substitute.

The clay pigeon and the trap which propels it at a terrific pace, are both the invention of Mr. George Ligowsky, of Cincinnati, who is a really representative sportsman and lover of a gun. He has worthily earned, not merely the barren honor of being the first to discover so good a substitute for live pigeon shooting, but he will undoubtedly reap a substantial reward in the near future.

Mr. Ligowsky has also, in experimenting in the manufacture of the clay saucer or pigeon, found a means by which pottery of any description can be moulded and shaped by machinery, instead of the hitherto only known method of hand labor, thereby insuring great regularity.

In the early time of shooting at this funny substitute for a bird, complaints were pretty general that, although a saucer may have been struck by many shots, oftimes *it was not broken*, which may, however, have arisen from other causes than irregularity of thickness of the clay ; such as *want of penetration* from insufficient or *bad powder* or *wads*, or from shells being imperfectly loaded with improper proportions of ammunition. Latterly, however, there has been such regularity in the manufacture of the clays, that if not broken when struck, the cause may be looked for elsewhere.

Having been for nearly fifty years an ardent lover of field sports and trap shooting, and having expended probably more money in pigeons than any person now living, and never having until recently shot at an inanimate object from a trap, I must confess to having felt a great objection to both glass balls and clay pigeons when first introduced, because I saw that the motion of the glass ball was *injurious to wing practice*, except that of course, it drew attention to the necessity of making certain calculations, and it also helped to give steadiness to the nerves in public shooting.

My first experience with the clay pigeon, about two years since, was an unfortunate one ; the traps being handled *by a novice*, acted so annoyingly that I gave it up in disgust, and did not see any more clays shot at until last summer.

From the few *proper shots* I saw made I was satisfied that the principle *was correct;* and having since had opportunity of seeing some shooting properly managed, I am satisfied now that it is *the thing of the future*, and that it will be very extensively in use this season.

Shooting from five traps, the plan I have very strenuously advocated, is certain to be generally adopted by representative sportsmen, and I notice the Ligowsky Co. offer special inducements in lowering the price of the traps in sets of five, or to complete the set. I hope, however, that the cost will be still further reduced, as I fail to see the necessity of throwing the birds at different elevations ; as if thrown at an elevation of about 20 feet at 40 yards from the trap, so that only the edge is exposed to the charge, it is *certainly all required.*

A record of 90 in 100, at 15 yards rise, in the third notch, with an elevation of 75 degrees, which presents almost a full view of the bird, and in which case the bird travels *much slower*, so as to be almost stationary at 30 yards, is not equal to a score of 70 with a good spring in the fourth notch and an elevation of 20 degrees.

For early practice I recommend *short rises* at clays, as they travel much faster than a bird, and make very difficult shooting at first ; a really good record can only be made with *great quickness* and *accuracy of aim.*

I was present lately at a public exhibition given by a celebrated shot, where the traps were so *manipulated* that it would be a farce to call it shooting, such as it was skill ; being somewhat equivalent to aiming at a

THE NATIONAL GUN ASSOCIATION. 59

miniature balloon at 30 yards; the bird being thrown almost perpendicular, consequently meeting the wind, it was almost standing still.

In any published report of a contest, in order to ascertain the degree of merit, a full account should be given of the *number of traps, how far apart, what notch, elevation at 40 yards*, and *at what rise*. Where these particulars are omitted the report is practically valueless, and is passed over as worthless by those most interested.

A few poles 20 feet high at 40 yards from the traps will show at a glance if the elevation is correct.

The following records may be interesting, if only for encouragement, and to show that great scores can be made with practice.

Dr. Carver and Captain Bogardus gave twenty-five exhibition shoots under the auspices of the Ligowsky Clay Pigeon Company. Conditions: 100 birds each, 18 yards rise, English rules, use of both barrels, traps fourth notch, as follows:

	CARVER.	BOGARDUS.
Chicago,	72	63
St. Louis,	85	69
Cincinnati,	89	74
Kansas City,	91	69
St. Joseph,	92	63
Leavenworth,	85	63
Omaha,	94	90
Council Bluffs,	96	96
Des Moines,	100	97
Davenport,	95	89
Burlington,	99	99
Quincy,	100	92
Peoria,	98	92
Terre Haute,	99	95
Indianapolis,	98	97
Dayton, O.,	94	94
Columbus,	76	93
Pittsburgh,	94	95
Philadelphia,	96	95
Jersey City,	98	94
New Haven,	96	82
Springfield, Mass.,	96	91
Worcester,	99	86
Providence,	92	94
Boston,	93	91
Totals,	2327	2163

Average: Carver, 93. Bogardus, 86.

Extract from Account of

First International Clay Pigeon Tournament,

CHICAGO, ILL., MAY 27-31, 1884.

Under the Auspices of

THE LIGOWSKY CLAY PIGEON CO.,
of Cincinnati, O.

Total Purses Distributed $4,000 — Principal Contest championship Match—Scores, Etc.

CHAMPIONSHIP TEAM SHOOT.

Teams of five men each. At ten single and five double clay pigeons, from five screened traps; singles, 18 yards rise, doubles, 15 yards rise. The individual making the best score to be entitled to the Ligowsky diamond badge. Referee, M. D. Gilman, af Worcester, Mass.; right judge, Anderson, of Denver, Col.; left judge, Folsom, of New Haven, Conn.; scorer, Houghton of Worcester, Mass.; assistant scorer, Limberg, of Cincinnati, Ohio. On the second day, F. Kimble, of Peoria, Ill., was substituted as right judge in place of Anderson.

BLUE ISLAND GUN CLUB, BLUE ISLAND, ILL.

Geo. Airey	01101 10101	00 00 10 00 10—8
G. Boeber	01011 01000	00 10 00 00 00—5
F. Bushnell	00011 00011	10 00 01 10 00—7
T. Igelhardt	10010 00111	00 10 10 11 00—9
L. Lichtenmeier	00010 01001	10 00 01 00 00—5—34

JACKSONVILLE GUN CLUB, JACKSONVILLE, ILL.

C. Henry	11110 01001	00 01 00 10 10—9
J. Stice	10111 01101	10 11 11 11 10-15
B. Sage	01100 01100	10 00 00 10 00—6
T. Taylor	00000 00011	10 00 10 11 11—8
C. Strong	10111 00001	11 10 01 10 00-10—48

CHICAGO SHOOTING CLUB, CHICAGO, ILL.

R. B. Wadsworth	11011 01111	11 01 01 11 01-15
M. J. Eich	10000 00001	11 10 00 01 10—7
Abe Kleinman	10110 10001	11 11 00 11 10-12
J. J, Gillespie	10110 01010	10 00 10 00 10—8
W. G. Payson	10100 01110	01 11 11 10 10-12—54

DIANA GUN CLUB, CHICAGO, ILL.

J. C. Muther	10000 11111	10 01 01 01 01–11	
Henry Ehlers	11101 00010	00 10 00 10 00— 7	
Powell Smith	11110 10000	10 00 11 10 11–11	
O. G. Eggen	00000 01001	01 00 10 10 10— 6	
Burmeister	01011 10011	00 00 10 00 00— 7	–42

BRADFORD SHOOTING CLUB, BRADFORD, PA.
(Team No. 2.)

W. H. Bradley	10100 01111	00 10 00 11 11–11	
W. L. Yelton	11000 01101	10 00 01 10 11–10	
A. B. Walker	00101 00110	10 00 10 11 10— 9	
I. W. Sherley	00110 00101	10 11 11 10 00–10	
C. H. McKevitt	11111 11111	10 01 10 10 00–14	–54

BRADFORD SHOOTING CLUB, BRADFORD, PA.
Team No. 1.)

F. Drake	10010 01000	01 10 11 01 01— 9	
Frank Gifford	00101 01110	10 10 10 10 01–10	
Alfred Smedley	00101 10000	01 10 11 01 00— 8	
John Denman	11001 11110	10 10 10 00 10–11	
J. C. Linneman	00101 10010	00 10 11 10 00— 8	–46

FARMINGTON SPORTING CLUB, FARMINGTON, ILL.

Geo. Woodruff	00010 00100	01 10 01 11 00— 7	
Jacob Brunner	01101 10010	00 11 10 01 10–10	
Taylor Anderson	10011 00010	10 00 00 10 11— 8	
Lewis Scales	11001 00100	00 10 10 00 10— 7	
Sam'l Caywood	01000 10100	00 00 10 00 11— 6	–33

CHIPPEWA GUN CLUB, CHIPPEWA FALLS, WIS.

J. A. Duncan	11101 11001	01 10 00 01 11–12	
Jos. Darlan	01000 10110	01 01 10 10 00— 8	
Sam'l Snyder	00201 00010	11 00 00 00 00— 4	
Robt. Kennedy	10010 10001	00 00 10 10 00— 6	
Jos. Herman	11111 10001	10 01 00 00 00–10	–40

KIRTLAND GUN CLUB, CLEVELAND, O.

C. F. Wheal	11001 10111	10 00 10 00 00— 9	
C. M. Roof	00100 00001	01 11 10 00 10— 7	
Alger	10001 10111	00 00 11 10 10–11	
Closse	11000 11101	01 10 10 10 10–11	
Eaton	00011 010$1	01 01 00 00 00— 7	–45

CAPITAL CITY GUN CLUB, WASHINGTON, D. C.

E. L. Mills	01001 11111	10 11 10 00 11–13	
Wm. Wagner	11000 01110	10 01 00 11 11–11	
W. B. McKeldon	01101 00100	11 10 11 10 10–11	
Jas. A. Bailey	11100 01100	01 01 00 01 01— 9	
Jas. H. Smith	11101 10000	00 00 10 00 00— 6	–50

WORCESTER SPORTSMEN'S CLUB, WORCESTER, MASS.

H. W. Eager	11110 00011	11 11 10 11 01–14	
E. T. Smith	10100 00011	00 11 11 00 10— 9	
G. A. Sampson	10010 11010	10 10 00 10 10— 9	
C. B. Holden	11111 01011	01 00 10 10 00–11	
W. S. Perry	10100 01110	01 11 10 11 11–13	–56

CLEVELAND GUN CLUB, CLEVELAND, O.

M. F. Silsby	10111 10110	10 10 01 10 00	—11
F. L. Chamberlain	10011 01100	01 11 11 11 11	—14
C. A. Calhoun	11011 00010	01 00 11 11 01	—11
D. C. Powers	00110 00111	00 00 11 01 10	— 9
R. E. Sheldon	11001 11010	11 11 11 11 01	—15—60

EXETER SPORTSMEN'S CLUB, EXETER, N. H.

Dr. C. H. Gerrish	11000 11110	11 11 10 11 01	—14
O. J. Jenkins	11111 01111	10 00 01 10 10	—13
A. F. Cooper	11011 11101	01 01 10 01 10	—13
C. M. Stark	11101 11110	10 11 11 10 11	—16
H. S. Taylor	11000 11000	11 11 01 10 11	—12—68

CINCINNATI INDEPENDENT SHOOTING CLUB, CINCINNATI, O.

A. Bandle	11110 00101	10 11 11 11 11	—15
J. E. Miller	11010 00000	10 00 01 11 00	— 7
Chas. Eckert	11111 10101	00 10 01 11 10	—13
Parker	11110 00010	11 01 00 11 10	—11
H. McMurchy	11111 00011	00 10 01 10 00	—10—56

Ties on fifty-six, at five singles, twenty-one yards rise, and two doubles, eighteen yards rise.

WORCESTER CLUB.

Eager	10010 01 10—4	Holden	01111 10 11— 7
Smith	00010 11 10—4	Perry	11111 10 11— 8
Sampson	10101 01 10—5		—
Total			28

CINCINNATI CLUB.

Bandle	01011 10 11—6	Parker	10110 10 01— 5
Miller	00100 11 00—3	McMurchy	declined to shoot
Eckert	00010 01 10—3		—
Total			17

Ties on fifty-four:

BRADFORD CLUB No. 2.

Yelton	01010 00 00—2	Sherley	10110 10 11— 6
Walker	00000 10 10—2	McKevitt	11010 11 11— 7
Bradley	01101 10 00—4		—
Total			21

CHICAGO CLUB.

Wadsworth	11100 10 01—5	Gillespie	10000 10 00— 1
Norton	10101 00 11—5	Wilson	01100 00 10— 3
Kleinmun	01111 11 10—7		—
Total			21

Exeter Club won first, $750.00, Cleveland second, Worcester third, Cincinnati fourth and Chicago and Bradford divided fifth. C. M. Stark of the Exeter Club won the individual diamond badge, $250.00, with a score of sixteen out of twenty. Mr. Stark shot a W. C. Scott & Son's Hammerless gun.

RECEPTION OF THE EXETER TEAM.

The citizens of Exeter, N. H., turned out to give the victorious team a fitting reception on their arrival from Chicago, Monday, June 2. The Exeter *News-Letter* describes it as follows :

" At 8 o'clock the band, accompanied by a large number of torch bearers, marched to the armory, where the members of Company D had assembled, and the procession was formed. They marched to the depot, where the team found on their arrival a large crowd gathered to welcome them home. Each member of the team was presented with a handsome bouquet, and they were placed in an open barouche drawn by four horses, and escorted in triumph to the square. The road was thronged with people, and their congratulations of the team were enlivened with the firing of crackers and cannon. The band played well, the soldier lads looked finely, the crowd was enthusiastic and the victorious marksmen were proud, tired and happy. Mr. Getchell can congratulate himself on the complete success of the affair, for not a single suggestion of addition or change in the programme could be thought of by the most confirmed grumbler that would not have marred the reception. When the procession reached the square in front of the Town Hall, they found a huge bonfire kindled, Mr. Hervey's house and G. Weston Leavitt's store was decorated with lanterns and the windows of the house filled with admiring spectators. The sidewalks were quickly filled with the crowd, and after the carriage containing the team had stopped in front of the Town Hall, Hon. John D. Lyman made the address as follows :

"GENTLEMEN OF THE EXETER SPORTSMEN'S CLUB : Welcome, thrice welcome home ! The military and citizens, yea, and the ladies come forth to bid you welcome as victors and rejoice with you over the blushing honors and triumphs won, while torches and illuminations fittingly light up these scenes of our congratulations. No emotion is more natural to generous souls than that which prompts them to welcome home the victors of heroic or artistic achievements. We come out to-night to welcome the victors, as the Greeks and Romans and every noble people of antiquity were wont to do. If the Greeks, the most cultured of all the ancient nations, and from off whose altars American Civilization is now daily plucking live coals to add to the brilliancy of its own enlightenment, thought it not unworthy to compute their time from eras marked by their sports and Olympian games, we may well heed their example in duly developing the wonderful physical powers with which a kind Heavenly Father has endowed us. Greece is scarcely better remembered for her Socrates and Demosthenes than for the marvelous skill of her citizens with bow and javelin. The chisel of Phidias is as immortal as the pen of Homer, and in sacred story the sling of David as the sayings of Solomon.

"Gentlemen, the art of shooting is the art of national defence. It is the art practiced so well by the heroes of the old French and Indian wars, some of whose headstones are hid from view very near where we now stand ; and again so well by Gen. Folsom and Light Infantry Poor and their comrades in the Revolution and the latter heroes of 1812 ; and never better than by those whose graves bear fresh decorations and the veterans who are here to welcome you to-night. Long, long may they live to enjoy the land they saved! Were not the barrier between these departed heroes of old and the living impassable, they might be here to-night to greet those who practice so well the art of shooting, by which they maintained the national liberty. As the law of Jehovah came forth from amid the thunder and lightning of Sinai, so liberty had her birth, and is maintained by the thunder and lightning of men who shoot. So far in this bloody world, shooting has seemed to be one of the fundamentally necessary arts, and the same steadiness of nerve and accuracy of sight that hits the glass balls in your contests will cause the nation's foes to fall at our country's call.

"Do good to those who hurt you,' say you, my good friend Chase. Well, no man on earth ever tortured me worse than you have, Dr. Gerrish. Now apply the good pastor's rule and say most earnestly, may your joy over this triumph of the skill of yourself and gentlemen of the club be as intense and far more lasting than was my anguish when you applied your remorseless steel to my strongly-rooted molars. Language can wish no greater.

"You, my friend Stark, won the diamond badge. Well, you could do no less and keep up the reputation of that Stark who taught the Indians of our wilds and the red coats at Bunker Hill, and both at Bennington, of his shooting qualities. You, Taylor, may proudly bear the name of him before whose shooting qualities the hosts of Mexico fled in despair. Cooper and Jenkins are worthy of such associates. At Concord bridge, a century since, a few patriots fired shots that were heard around the world as quickly as horses and sails could speed, but Jove flashed your victory over continents and under oceans in the twinkling of an eye. In presence of this vast audience, standing close by the historic spot where the first government upon the American continent in independence of the mother country was instituted, facing the venerable building where Washington was entertained, near by the resting place of heroes of the old and recent times, and in the presence of veterans from battles as nobly fought as any in the annals of time, we pray that your success, gentlemen, in all noble enterprises may be as great as that of your shooting at Chicago.

"Dr. Charles H. Gerrish responded on the part of the club :

"I thank you for the kind reception you have accorded us on our return from Chicago, and can assure you this welcome is for us the proudest feature of our trip. We left here a week ago last Saturday, as you all know, to represent the Exeter Sportsmen's Club at the Ligowsky Clay Pigeon Match at Chicago. At Worcester we met the club from that city and continued in their company until we left them at Worcester on our return. And let me pause here to pay these gentlemen a well-deserved tribute for the large part they contributed toward making our visit and our journey pleasant. Their kindly wishes for our success and their cordial congratulations when success was achieved, will long be remembered by each of us, side by side with this flattering reception you have accorded us,

We arrived safely in Chicago, and put up at the Palmer House, where many of the clubs made their headquarters. Tuesday the wind blew a gale, so it was decided to postpone the shoot until the next day. Wednesday morning when I arose I raised the curtain and saw a pennant standing out straight from its staff with the force of the wind. I turned to my room mates—I may remark there were three of us in the room—and said, 'Boys, it blows like the devil. Our chances are good.' We shot and scored thirty-five. It was not a large score—it was a very poor score, not one of the teams who were present would have accepted. They would rather have shot. Yet when the thirteenth team had finished, thirty-five led the list. The next morning when I arose I looked out of the window and saw that same pennant standing out as flat as a pancake. 'Boys,' said I, ' It is blowing hard. We have a good chance.' We shot and scored thirty-three. It was not a great score. No team present would have accepted it, yet it was enough. The team has taken in prizes over $1,400 in the tournament, including the grand prize of $750 and the diamond badge awarded to the best individual score, valued at $250. I thank you in the name of the team for your welcome home, and hope that in future your welcome will be just as cordial whether we come as victors or vanquished.

"At the conclusion of the doctor's speech, he asked Mr. Stark to arise and let the people see the diamond badge won by him at the tournament. He at once arose, amid the cheers of the large assemblage, and the badge, which was fastened to the white satin ribbon by which Mr. Stark gained admittance to the field, was plainly seen attached to the lapel of his coat.

"The badge is of fine gold with a large diamond in the center, surrounded by a laurel wreath finished in colors. On the top is a pigeon with extended wings, also finished in color. It was made for the Ligowsky Clay Pigeon Co. On the reverse side is the inscription :

DONATED BY THE
LIGOWSKY CLAY PIGEON CO., OF CINCINNATI, O.,
To C. M. STARK,
EXETER SPORTSMEN'S CLUB,
INDIVIDUAL CHAMPIONSHIP.
1ST INT. C. P. TOURNAMENT, CHICAGO, MAY, 1884.

" At the close of the tournament it was at the option of Mr. Stark to take the badge or $250 in cash. He took the badge.

The barouche containing the team was then escorted to the store of Mr. Getchell where they alighted, and the crowd slowly dispersed. At 10:30 the Sportsmen's Club entertained the team and a few friends at Hervey's, where a sumptuous repast was served, and an hour was agreeably spent in hearing pleasant reminiscences ot the Chicago tournament. Regret was expressed by all present that Mr. Hervey could not entertain a larger number at this time, so that the club could have made the invitations more general.

EXTRACTS FROM PRESS ACCOUNTS

OF THE

Second International Clay-Pigeon Tournament.

New Orleans, La., February 11th to 16th, 1885.

THE INTERNATIONAL TEAM CHAMPIONSHIP MATCH.

The weather was bitter cold from 9 o'clock in the morning, when the shooting began, until late at night. That portion of ground on which the shooting was done resembled a camp in war times; a large fire burned to keep the shooters warm, hundreds of shotguns stood against the stands, while boxes upon boxes of loaded shells were piled up for use in the match. Throughout the day firing continued, and the voice of the shooter crying "pull" was followed by the sudden rise of a brick-colored object, which was winged in its flight by the aim of the marksman, and flew in pieces over the ground. The slaughter of clay pigeons was fearful to behold. It was an interesting scene, and the celebrated shots seemed to enjoy the sport throughout.

February 12. *Conditions.*—Open to teams of three men belonging to any organized club; entrance $25 per team; 10 singles and 5 pairs of double clay pigeons, 5 traps; 4 moneys—40, 30, 20, 10 per cent.; 18 yards rise for singles, 16 yards for doubles. The first special prize was a Spencer repeating shotgun, value $100, presented by the Spencer Repeating Arms Co., of Windsor, Conn., for the best individual score made. The judges and referee in this match were: J. R. Stice, of Jacksonville, Ill., left judge; A. Cardona, New Orleans, La., right judge; and A. Meaders, of Nashville, referee.

BOSTON GUN CLUB—TEAM NO. 1.

H. W. Eager.................11100 11010—6   10 10 10 10 10—5—11
W. S. Perry.................10110 01110—6   10 11 10 11 11—8—14
O. R. Dickey................11101 11101—8   11 01 01 10 11—7—15

  Total..40

CINCINNATI GUN CLUB

B. Tiepel ....11111 10111—9   10 10 10 10 11—6—15
A. Bandle...................11010 00111—6   00 10 10 10 10—4—10
H. McMurchy.................10111 11011—8   10 11 11 01 10—7—15

  Total 40

BOSTON GUN CLUB—TEAM NO. 2.

W. L. Davis.................11110 10010—6   01 10 10 10 01—5—11
C. M. Stark ....11011 01110—7   11 10 11 10 11—8—15
J. S. Sawyer................11111 11111-10   10 00 10 11 00—4—14

  Total..40

CENTRAL OHIO SHOOTING ASSOCIATION, OF SPRINGFIELD, OHIO.

T. Gastright	10111	01010—6	10 11 10 10 11—7—13
C. E. Verges	01011	01011—6	10 10 11 10 10—6—12
L. E. Russell	01111	00001—5	11 01 11 11 10—8—13

Total..38

HOUSTON GUN CLUB.

A. Erichson	00001	11100—4	10 10 10 10 11—6—10
W. W. Holland	11100	11100—6	11 00 10 11 01—6—12
H. A. Penrose	11110	01011—7	11 10 10 11 11—8—15

Total..37

KANSAS CITY GUN CLUB.

J. E. Riley	00000	01111—4	11 10 01 10 00—5—9
F. Erb	10010	00111—5	10 01 10 10 11—6—11
J. A. R. Elliott	10010	10011—5	11 10 00 01 01—5—10

Total..30

Ties on forty for first, second, and third moneys:

BOSTON GUN CLUB—TEAM NO. 1. | CINCINNATI GUN CLUB.
Eager .... 11110 00 11—6 | Tiepel .... 11101 11 10—7
Perry .... 01110 10 11—6 | Bandle .... 01101 00 00—3
Dickey .... 11011 01 11—7—10 | McMurchy ..... 10001 11 11—6—16

BOSTON GUN CLUB—TEAM NO. 2.
Davis .... 10011 00 10—4 | Sawyer .... 11011 10 10—6—16
Stark .... 10101 01 11—6 |

Boston Gun Club, Team No. 1, won first money.

Second tie on 16 for second and third moneys:

CINCINNATI GUN CLUB. | BOSTON GUN CLUB—TEAM NO. 2.
Tiepel .... 01111 10 11—7 | Davis 11011 00 10
Bandle .... 11011 10 11—7 | Stark 11111 00w
McMurchy ..... 11110 11 00—6—20 | Sawyer .... 11011 w

Cincinnati Gun Club won second money; Boston Gun Club, Team No. 2, won third; Central Ohio Shooting Association won fourth.

Ties of 15 (individual scores) for Spencer shotgun:

McMurchy ...... 01011—3 w | Tiepel .... 11110—4 11 11—8
Dickey .... 10111—4 11 10—7 | Penrose .... 11010—3 w
Stark .... 10110—3 w |

B. Tiepel, of Cincinnati, won the Spencer repeating rifle.

THE INTERNATIONAL INDIVIDUAL CHAMPIONSHIP MATCH.

February 16. *Conditions.*—Open to the world. Entrance, $10; at 10 single clay pigeons, 18 yards, and 5 pairs of doubles, 15 yards; entrance purses to be divided into 3 prizes—75, 15, 10 per cent. First prize $250 cash or the Diamond Championship Badge (guaranteed by the Ligowsky Clay Pigeon Co.), won by C. M. Stark, of Exeter, N. H., at the First International Clay Pigeon Tournament, at Chicago, May, 1884. Mr. Stark returned the badge; so the first prize was the badge. Special prize: To the best score, one heavy Henry Richards single-barrel gun, donated by J. P. Moor's Sons, of New York.

```
W. E. Watkins...Nashville, Tenn...11110    11011—8    10 11 11 10  01—7—15
J. C. Lineman,...Bradford, Pa........11111    01110—8    11 01 11 10  01—7—15
Geo. Essig.......Plattsburg, Mo....10001    01000—3    10 00 01 10  00—3— 6
H. McMurchy....Cincinnati, O.....11111    11111—8    10 11 11 10  11—8—16
A. Bandle........Cincinnati, O.....10111    00110—6    10 10 11 11  11—8—14
A. Meaders......Nashville, Tenn...11110    11110—8    01 11 01 11  11—8—16
F. L. Chamberlin.Cleveland, O.....01011    11110—7    11 11 10 10  00—6—13
C. M. Stark......Winchester, Mass.11001    01100—5    11 11 11 11  11-10—15
W. S. Perry......Worcester, Mass..11110    01000—5    10 10 01 10  10—5—10
H. W. Eager.....Marlborough, Mass11011    11111—9    00 10 01 10  10—4—13
B. Tiepel ......  Covington, Ky ...01111    01111—8    11 11 11 10  10—8—16
J. R. Stice........Jacksonville, Ill..  11111    10011—8    10 11 10 10  00—5—13
E. Voris .........Crawfordsville, Ind11110    11011—8    11 10 10 00  10—5—13
C. E. Verges......Lowell, O........01100    00111—5    01 10 11 10  11—7—12
O. R. Dickey.....Boston, Mass.....11011    01111—8    10 11 11 11  10—8—16
Jas. Lawrence ....New York, N. Y..10010    00001—3    11 11 11 10  00—7—10
J. Tuttle..........Natchez, Miss...  01111    01011—7    10 10 01 00  00—3—10
Jno. Judd.........New Albany, Ind.01110    10001—5    11 10 10 11  11—8—13
A. H. Bogardus...Elkhart, Ill......  11010    01111—7    01 10 11 10  10—6—13
W. F. Carver.....New Haven, Conn.11111    11111—9    10 11 10 10  11—7—16
Fred Erb.........Kansas City, Mo..01111    10101—7    11 10 10 00  11—5—12
Den ..............................01000    11101—5    00 00 00 01  11—3— 8
W. F. Cody......North Platte, Neb.11101    01100—6    11 10 01 11  11—8—14
Geo. W. Bookout.Vicksburg, Miss..10100    01111—6    11 01 10 11  10—7—13
T. Gastright......Covington, Ky ...10110    11011—7    10 10 10 10  11—6—13
D. Kirkwood .....Boston, Mass.....11011    10101—7    01 00 01 10  10—4—11
J. A. R. Elliott....Grenola, Kan ....01110    11011—7    10 11 11 11  11—9—16
```

Ties of 16, shot off at 5 singles and 2 pairs:

```
McMurchy... ......00111    11 11—7 | Dickey.............00111    01 10—5
Meaders ...........10011    11 01—6 | Carver.............00111    10 10—5
Tiepel ..............11111    10 10—7 | Elliott .............00010    10w
```

Second tie:

```
McMurchy.........00111    11 11—7 | Tiepel ........11111    10 10—7
```

Third tie:

```
McMurchy.........01111    11 11—8 | Tiepel ........11011    11 11—8
```

Fourth tie:

```
McMurchy.........11101    00w     | Tiepel ........11100    11 10—6
```

B. Tiepel won First, Diamond Badge; H. M. McMurchy won second.

Tie for fourth and fifth:

```
Carver. ............11111    10 10—7 | Dickey............01110    01w
```

W. F. Carver won fourth, O. R. Dickey won fifth.

The match was called at 1:30 P. M., and proved to be the most interesting and exciting contest, not only of this tournament, but also of any previous contest ever held in this country, the best shots of the entire United States being represented, including Dr. Carver and Capt. Bogardus.

McMurchy, Meaders, Tiepel, Dickey, Dr. Carver, and Elliott tied on a score of 16 out of a possible 20. The tie was shot off at five singles and two pairs doubles, handicap of three yards, resulting in a tie for first place between Tiepel and McMurchy, of Cincinnati, Meaders next, with a tie between Dr. Carver and Dickey for fourth and fifth places. The race between McMurchy and Tiepel was most exciting. On the ties shot off, they tied twice, and the third time it was decided in favor of Tiepel, who thus won the diamond championship badge. The shoot off between Dickey and Carver was decided in favor of the latter. It was the universal opinion that this match was the most interesting ever held in this country, on account of the fact that the acknowledged two champions of the world, as well as the champions of eleven States, participated therein.

The subjoined table gives the guns and charges used by the contestants in the above matches:

Name and Address.	Make of Gun.	Bore of Gun.	Weight of Gun.	Length of Barrel.	Kind of Powder	Charge in Drams.	Kind and Size of Shot.	Charge in Ounces.
A. Kenner, New Orleans	Saget.	12	7lb	32in	B	3	Pittsburgh No. 5.	1⅛
Henry Peters, Cincinnati	Parker.	10	9½	30	B	4	Pittsburgh No. 5.	1¼
Chas. E. Strawn, Jacksonville, Ill	E. C. Green . . .	10	11½	34	B	4	Chilled.	1¼
J. S. Sawyer, Cambridge, Mass .	Kirkwood	10	10½	32	B	4½	Tatham No. 7 . .	1¼
J. Henry Weyer, Augusta, Ga .	Colts.	10	9½	32	B	5	Tatham No. 8 . .	1¼
B. Newell, Boston Mass.	Schaeffer.	10	9	30	B	4¼	Ch. No. 8 Trap. .	1¼
J. Tuttle, Natchez, Miss	H. & R.	10	10	32	B	4¼	Ch. No. 7 Trap .	1¼
C. E. Bardwell, Tekamah, Neb .	Parker.	10	10	32	W	5	No. 8 Chilled . .	1⅛
Jno. M. Auter, Vicksburg, Miss .	Parker.	10	9¼	30	B	4¼	No. 7 Chilled . .	1¼
H. W. Eager, Marlboro, Mass . .	W. & C. Scott . .	10	9½	32	B	4¼	Leroy No. 7. . .	1⅛
A. T. Lucius, Houston, Tex. . .	H. & R.	10	9½	30	B	5	No. 7 Chilled . .	1¼
H. R. Downey, Houston, Tex. .	Daly	10	9¾	30	B	5	No. 7 Chilled . .	1¼
W. B. Ralston, Blue Ball, O. . .	Scott.	10	9.2	31	B	4¼	No. 7.	1¼
J. E. Riley, Kansas City, Mo . .	William & Powell.	10	11	32	H		Tatham	1¼
I. W. Shirley, Bradford, Pa. . .	Daly	10	10	32	B	4½	Tatham	1¼
J. A. R. Elliott, Grenola, Kan. .	H. & R.	10	11	32	H		Tatham No. 8 . .	1¼
Geo. B. Dougan, Leadville Colo.	Scott & Son . . .	10	9	30		4	No. 8.	1⅛
A. T. White, Tekamah, Neb. . .	Baker	10	9¼	30	W	4	Chilled No. 8 . .	1⅛
Geo. W. Bookout, Vicksburg, Miss	H. & R.	10	9½	30	B	4½	St. Louis Ch. No. 7	1¼
H. G. Seeligson, Houston, Tex .	E. Whistler. . . .	10	11	32		5	No. 8	
E. T. Owens, Natchez, Miss. . .	Westley Richards.	10	9¼	30	B	4½	Chilled No. 8. . .	
C. E. Verges, Lowell, O	Bonehill	10	10	32	B	4½	Chilled No. 8. . .	1¼
John Judd, New Albany, Ind . .	Greener	12	9	30	B	4	No. 7	1⅛
J. Leicht, Liberty, Texas	Spencer Rep. . .	12	8¼	30	W	1	No. 8	1¼
Howard Gove, Galena, Kan . . .	E. C. Green . . .	10	9½	32	B	4½	Hard No. 7 . . .	1¼
H. L. Foote, Rolling Fork, Miss.	J. A. Nichols. . .	10	9½	30	B	4½	St. Louis No. 7 .	1¼
Geo. Essig, Plattsburg, Mo . . .	H. & R.	12	8⅛	30	B	4	Tatham No. 8 . .	1¼
Jas. Lawrence, New York. . . .	W. & C. Scott . .	10	9	30½	W	4	Chilled No. 7 . .	1¼
F. A. Cousin, New Orleans . . .	Greener	10	10	33	B	4	Tatham Ch. No. 8	1¼
F. L. Chamberlain, Cleveland, O.	Westley Richards	10	9.3	31	B	4½	No. 8 Chilled . .	1¼
W. L. Davis, Boston.	Scott Hammerless	10	10	30	B	4	No. 7	1¼
O. R. Dickey, Boston	Scott Hammerless	10	9¼	32	B	3¼	Tatham No. 6 . .	1¼
Fred. Erb, Jr., Kansas City. . .	Daly.	10	10	32		5	Kansas City No. 8	1¼
Albert Erichson, Houston, Tex .	Westley Richards	10	9½	30			. . . .	
Al. Bandle, Cincinnati.	Parker.	10	9¼	30	B		Chilled No. 8 . .	1¼
Jas. N. Frye, Boston.	Schafer.	10	9½	30	B	4	Tatham Ch. No. 7	1¼
De Fuentes, New Orleans, La . .	Greener	10	9½	31		4	No. 8.	1¼
T. Gastright, Cincinnati. . . .	Parker.	10	11	32	B	3½	No. 7.	1¼
W. W. Holland, Texas.	Webly	10	11	30	W	5	Chilled No. 8 . .	1¼
Wm. Mayronne, New Orleans. .	Parker.	10	9½	32	H	4	Chilled No. 8 . .	1¼
H. McMurchy, Cincinnati. . . .	H. & R. Ham'rless	10	10	32	B	4½	Pittsburgh No. 8.	1¼
Frank S. Parmelee, Omaha, Neb.	Daly.	10	10¼	32	B	5	Chilled No. 7 . .	1¼
H. A. Penrose, San Angela, Tex.	Scott Hammerless	10	9½	32			. . . .	1¼
Wm. S. Perry, Worcester, Mass.	Parker.	10	10	34		4	Chilled No. 7 . .	1¼
Dr. L. E. Russell, Springfield, O.	Scott & Son . . .	10	9½	30	B	4¼	No. 7 Trap. . . .	1¼
J. Z. Scott, Jacksonville, Ill. . .	E. E. Green . . .	10	11¼	34	B	4½	Chicago No. 7 . .	1¼
C. M. Stark, Boston, Mass. . . .	Scott Hammerless	10	9½	32	O	4½	Tatham Ch. No. 8	1¼
J. R. Stice, Jacksonville, Ill. . .	E. C. Green . . .	10	11¼	34	B	4½	Chicago No. 7 . .	1¼
E. E. Stubbs, Gainesville, Ark. .	Spencer	12	7	32	W	4	Chicago No. 7 . .	1⅛
Ben Tiepel, Cincinnati, O	Parker.	10	10¼	32	B	3½	Chilled No. 7 . .	1¼
Ed. Voris, Crawfordsville, Ind. .	Green	10	9	30	B	4¾	Pittsburgh. . . .	1¼
A. S. Wakely, Milford, Mich . .	Richards.	10	9¾	30	B	5	Chilled No. 8 . .	1¼
A. W. West, Parkersburg, W. Va.	Scott Hammerless	10	10¼	32	D	4¼	Chilled No. 8 . .	1¼
W. E. Watkins, Nashville, Tenn.	Daly.	10	10¼	32	D'	5½	Chilled No. 8 . .	1¼

In the column headed "Kind of Powder," B indicates Black Powder; W, Wood Powder; H, Hazard; O, Oriental Falcon; D, Dead; D', Dupont's Black,

The Cincinnati team, all used 10 gauge guns, F F F G, black powder, and 1¼ ounces of Pittsburgh No. 8 chilled shot to the load. McGraw, Gastright and Bandle loaded with 4 drams of powder; McMurchy with 4½ drams; and Teipel with 3½ drams. Bandle used a No. 10 thick felt Eley wad between the powder and the shot, and the other four used two No. 9 black-edged or pink-edged wads between powder and shot; while all used a split black-edged wad on top of the shot, in a U. M. C. paper cartridge crimped. Teipel's gun weighed 10½; McGraw and Bandle's, each 9½; McMurchy's, 10; and Gastright's, 11 pounds.

ANNOUNCEMENT FOR THE FUTURE.

THE JULY TELEGRAPHIC MATCH.

OPEN ONLY TO MEMBERS OF THE NATIONAL GUN ASSOCIATION.

JULY 4, 1885, 3 P. M.

And Every Succeeding July 4th Thereafter.

Conditions.—National Gun Association Rules to govern. Ten single Ligowsky clay pigeons and five pairs doubles. Entrance fee $1.00, to be sent by mail so as to reach the undersigned at any time preceding the shoot. Four moneys. Prize: To the best score the National Badge (in gold, value $10.00), donated by this Association. At the above time and date, any member desiring to compete, shall repair to any shooting ground and shoot the above score, accompanied by the President and Secretary of his gun club, or by any two members of this Association. He shall telegraph his score the same day, by day or night message; and shall also mail the score, certified by either of the above two as being correct, stating also the time and place of the shoot. Ties will be decided by a similar match, with the additional 3-yards handicap, 20 days thereafter, viz., July 24, 3 P. M.

Those members who, through carelessness, or for other reasons, may have failed to remit the entrance fee in due time by mail, can still enter by mailing $1.00 before 1 P. M., and by telegraphing per day message not later than 1 P. M., July 4, substantially as follows: "Mailed dollar entrance July Telegraphic Match." Any person not a member, desiring to compete, shall mail, before 1 P. M., July 4, the $5 initiation members' fee in addition to the above, and shall telegraph: "Mailed six dollars, membership and entrance July Telegraphic match."

Members will shoot at their permanent handicap. Any one who has not established a handicap record shall shoot his singles at 18 yards and doubles at 15 yards.

The Executive Committee shall duly announce the result, and act upon all points in controversy. Address all communications to

J. E. BLOOM,
Treas. Nat. Gun Ass'n,
Cincinnati, O.

The Most Enticing Programme ever offered.

FIRST INTER-STATE

Shot-Gun Wing-Shooting Tournament,

— UNDER THE AUSPICES OF —

THE NATIONAL GUN ASSOCIATION,

TO BE HELD AT THE "FAIR GROUNDS."

Springfield, O., May 5, 6, 7, 8, & 9, 1885.

PRIZES, $2,000.00, GUARANTEED.

EXECUTIVE COMMITTEE.

CAPT. A. H. BOGARDUS, Elkhart, Ills.
J. E. BLOOM, Cincinnati, O.
Dr. L. E. RUSSELL, Springfield, O.

Assisted by the following Officers and Members of

THE CENTRAL OHIO SHOOTING ASSOCIATION.

CHAS. WENDT, Kenton, O.	WARREN LEFFEL, Springfield, O.
A. E MESSERLEY, Greenville, O.	C. C. LANE, Bellefontaine, O.
WM. ACKERMAN, Lima, O.	C. C. KIRKPATRIC, Springfield, O.
MONROE HALL, Greenville, O.	Dr. H. H. SEYS, "
N. S. WEAVER, Kenton, O.	J. F. HAMILTON, "
J. H. HORNBERGER, Bellefontaine, O.	A. MCWILSON, "
W. B. RALSTON, Blue Ball, O.	A. J. SLACH, "
AL. BANDLE, Cincinnati, O.	H. F. ROBINSON, Cincinnati, O.
JAS. RITTY, Dayton, O.	A. SANDERS, Dayton, O.

SPRINGFIELD'S CITIZENS RECEPTION COMMITTEE:

H. L. ROCKAFELD,	JOHN KINNANE,
JOHN COHAN,	D. W. STROUD,
A. W. BUTT,	W. R. BURNETT.

SPECIAL ACCOMMODATION FOR LADIES.

ADMISSION, 25c.   -   -   To GRAND STAND, 50c.

All Matches to be shot under the Rules of

THE NATIONAL GUN ASSOCIATION.

COPIES FOR SALE AT THE BOX OFFICE.

Matches open to members only; parties so desiring can become members by applying to either of the Executive Committee on the grounds.

SPECIAL NOTICE.—Non-members can obtain the privileges of members for this Tournament only upon payment of two dollar and subject to the same penalties and restrictions.

⇢ SHOOTING FROM 9.30 A. M., to 6 P. M. ⇠

Besides the main 5 traps, two additional sets of traps will be constantly at the disposal of the shooters, where the entrance fees will be $2.00 and $1.00 respectively.

Where Matches with Live Birds are announced, when the latter can not possibly be obtained, Ligowsky Clay Pigeons will be substituted.

—— SPECIAL PRIZE, $100, ——

Donated by the National Gun Association for the best general average scores in Matches No. 2, 3, 4, 5, 6, 7, ˋ, 11, 12, 13, 15, 16, 18, 19, which may properly be designated the Consolidated Contest or C. C.

For the First Best Average in the Consolidated Contest,	$40
" " Second " " " " "	$30
" " " Poorest " " " "	$20
" " Poorest " " " "	$10

Messrs. Bailey, Farrell & Co., Pittsburgh, Pa., have kindly donated 6 bags of their No. 8 Trap Shot, to the three best scores in this match, viz: 3 to First, 2 to Second; 1 to Third.

FIRST DAY.

MATCH No. 1 —Individual Handicap Sweepstake.
   Seven Single Clay Pigeons.   Entrance, $5.00.

MATCH No. 2.—Individual Handicap Sweepstake.   Prizes, $100.
   Seven Single Clay Pigeons.   Entrance, $5.00.
   Guaranteed Prizes: First, $40; Second, $30; Third, $20; Fourth, $10.

MATCH No. 3.—Individual Handicap.   Prizes, $100.
   Seven Single Live Pigeons.   Entrance, $5.00.
   Guaranteed Prizes: First, $40; Second, $30; Third, $20; Fourth, $10.

MATCH No. 4.—Individual Handicap.   Prize, $100.
   Five Pairs Double Clay Pigeons.   Entrance, $5.00.
   Guaranteed Prizes: First, $40; Second, $30; Third, $20; Fourth, $10.

MATCH No. 5.—Twin-Team Handicap.   Prize, $150.
   Open to any team of two; each member to shoot 5 singles.
   Entrance, $10.00.
   Guaranteed Prizes: First, $60; Second, $40; Third, $30; Fourth, $20.

SECOND DAY.

MATCH No. 6.—Individual Handicap. Prizes, $100.
    Seven Single Clay Pigeons. Entrance, $5.00.
    Guaranteed Prizes: First, $40; Second, $30; Third, $20; Fourth, $10.

MATCH No. 7.—Individual Handicap. Prizes, $100.
    Seven Single Live Pigeons. Entrance, $5.00.
    Guaranteed Prizes: First, $40; Second, $30; Third, $20; Fourth, $10.

MATCH No. 8.—Individual Handicap. Prizes, $200.
    Twenty-Five Single Clay Pigeons. Entrance, $10.00.
    Guaranteed Prizes: First, $80; Second, $60; Third, $40; Fourth $20.

MATCH No. 9.—Inter-State Club-Team Championship.
    Sweepstake open to any Club-Team of three, all being residents of the same State.
    Ten Single Clay Pigeons, Five Pairs Double. Entrance $15 per team; three purses, 50%, 30%, 20%.

MATCH No. 10.—Miss and Out Sweepstake. Entrance, $2.00.

THIRD DAY.

MATCH No. 11.—Individual Handicap. Prize, $100.
    Seven Single Clay Pigeons. Entrance, $5.00.
    Guaranteed Prizes: First, $40; Second, $30; Third, $20; Fourth, $10.

MATCH No. 12.—Individual Handicap. Prize, $150.
    Five Single Live Pigeons, Two Pairs Double. Entrance, $7.00
    Guaranteed Prizes: First, $50; Second, $40; Third, $30; Fourth, $10.

THE DIAMOND BADGE MATCH; Individual Handicap.

MATCH No. 13.—Prize, The Diamond Badge or $250.
    Ten Single Clay Pigeons; Five Pairs Double. Entrance, $10.00.
    Guaranteed Prize, to the best Individual Score.

THE DIAMOND BADGE,

(Intrinsic value, $290) won by C. M. Stark of Exeter, N. H., at the First International Clay Pigeon Tournament, Chicago, Ills., May, 1884; presented for redemption, and won by B. Teipel of Covington, Ky, at the Second International Clay Pigeon Tournament, New Orleans, La., Feb.'85. Should said Badge not be presented for redemption at the time of this Match, the Association guarantees the first prize to be $250 cash. The Association further guarantees to redeem said Badge from present winner for $250 cash within one year from date.

MATCH No. 14.—Non-Winners' Individual Handicap. Prizes, $75.
    Seven Single Clay Pigeons. Entrance, $5.00.
    Guaranteed Prizes: First, $30; Second, $20; Third, $15; Fourth, $10.

FOURTH DAY.

MATCH No. 15.—The "Bogardus Cup" Championship Match.
The Official Scores of which will also be accepted for the competition for

THE CHAMBERLIN CARTRIDGE CO'S PRIZES, $2000.

Conditions: Fifty Single Clay Pigeons, and Twenty-Five Pairs Double Clay Pigeons.

The Singles only will be shot to-day; the doubles to-morrow. Entrance. $5.00.

Guaranteed Prizes: First, The "Bogardus Cup" and $25; Second, Third, Fourth each $10; balance to "Cup Fund" and the Association.

The Cup shall be again submitted for competition under similar conditions at each Tournament of the Association during the years 1885-6. The winner making the maximum scores in said years, shall be entitled to hold the cup subject to challenge, as set forth below.

Final ties between winners at successive Tournaments shall be decided at time and place indicated by the Association.

After the Final Inter-State Tournament of 1886, the Cup shall be held subject to challenge under the following

— RULES GOVERNING —

THE

"BOGARDUS CUP."

1. The final winner of the cup shall give a satisfactory guarantee to Captain A. H. Bogardus for the safety thereof, in the shape of a responsible surety.

2. The winner shall pledge himself to shoot any challenger, for a sum not less than $100 a side within two months of the date of said challenge, under penalty of forfeiting said cup.

3. Any party challenging the holder of this Cup shall make a deposit of $50, as a forfeit for a match of $100 a side, in the hands of the secretary of the National Gun Association. to be covered by the challenged party with an equal amount. The balance of the money $50 a side. shall be deposited in the same hands three days before the match is shot; the match then becomes "play or pay". In case of the holder not complying with the foregoing conditions, he shall forfeit the cup to the party challenging.

4. Every contestant for this cup shall pledge himself to contend for the same under the Trap-Shooting Rules of

THE NATIONAL GUN ASSOCIATION,

And make all necessary arrangements, and furnish the Clay Pigeons. Each party to pay half the expenses of the same, and if gate money be charged, it shall be divided equally.

5. All matches for this cup shall be at one hundred single and 50 doubles each.

6. The holder of this cup shall name the place where the same shall be contested for.

7. If the party holds this Cup for two years against all comers it shall become his personal property.

8. Where practical so to do. the match shall be shot under the auspices of the National Gun Association, at the place and time designated by the latter.

MATCH No. 16.—Individual Handicap. Prizes, $100.
    Seven Single Clay Pigeons. Entrance, $5 00.
    Guaranteed Prize: First, $40; Second, $30; Third, $20; Fourth $10.

MATCH No. 17.—Non-Winners' Handicap. Prizes, $100.
    Five Single Clay Pigeons Entrance, $5 00,
    Guaranteed Prize: First, $40; Second, $30; Third, $20; Fourth, $10.

FIFTH DAY.

MATCH No. 15.—Continued for the Bogardus Cup and The Chamberlin Cartridge Co's Prizes.

MATCH No 18.—Individual Handicap. Prizes, $100.
    Seven Single Live Pigeons. Entrance. $5.00
    Guaranteed Prizes: First, $40; Second, $30; Third, $20; Fourth $10.

MATCH No. 19—Individual Handicap. Prizes, $100.
    Three Pairs Live Pigeons. Entrance, $5.00
    Guaranteed Prizes: First, $40; Second $30; Third, $20; Fourth, $10.

MATCH No. 20.—Non-Winners' Handicap. Prize, $100.
    Five Single Live Pigeons. Entrance, $5.00.
    Guaranteed Prizes: First, $40; Second $30; Third, $20; Fourth, $10.

HEAD-QUARTERS IN SPRINGFIELD.

ARCADE HOTEL, $2 00 per day.
    LAGONDA HOUSE, $1.50 per day.
        ST. JAMES HOTEL, $1.00 per day.

RAIL ROADS FROM SPRINGFIELD.

The Indiana, Bloomington and Western R R., with connections for all points West at Peoria Ills. and the Decatur Branch for the South-West; connections at Indianapolis, with Chicago and the North-West.

The Pittsburgh, Cin'ti and St. Louis Ry. for East and South.

The C. C. C. and I. Ry. for the South and North.

The N. Y., Penn. and Ohio Ry., for N. Y., and the East.

Excursion rates: pay full rates going and 1 cent per mile returning, upon presenting a certificate signed by the National Gun Association.

Captain A. H. BOGARDUS,

Champion Wing Shot of the World,

Will undertake daily, at 4 P. M., to break 300 Ligowsky Clay Pigeons, thrown from 5 traps, within 20 minutes. He will use three different Guns, viz: 10 *Gauge, weight,* 9¼ *lbs.;* 12 *Gauge, weight,* 7½ *lbs.;* 20 *Gauge, weight,* 5½ *pounds.*

AN INTER-STATE TOURNAMENT,

—— Under the Auspices of ——

THE NATIONAL GUN ASSOCIATION,

—— Will be held in the City of ——

Cleveland, Ohio, October 5 to 10, 1885,

Where all the ties for the CHAMBERLIN CARTRIDGE Co.'s PRIZES will be finally decided.

FIRST INTERNATIONAL TOURNAMENT,

Under the Auspices of

THE NATIONAL GUN ASSOCIATION,

Washington, D. C., May, 1886.

All sportsmen and citizens alike, are invited to join the NATIONAL GUN ASSOCIATION. Initiation Fee, $5.00, payable, if desired, in monthly installments of $1.00. Annual dues, $1.00, payable upon entering, and thereafter on May 1st.

Send five 2-cent stamps for Book on Constitution, Trap Shooting Rules, etc., to the Secretary of the N. G. A., Box 1292, Cincinnati, O.

The members of the National Gun Association are requested to meet at 8 P. M., May 4th (Monday), for the transaction of such business as may be brought before them, at Arcade Hotel.

The 80-page Hand Book of The National Gun Association, containing Constitution, Trap Shooting Rules, etc , can be ordered through any News Dealer, from any "News Company". Price, 10 cents.

Where to Buy
Where to Hunt!
Where to Fish!

THE AMERICAN SPORTSMAN'S

DIRECTORY

—AND—

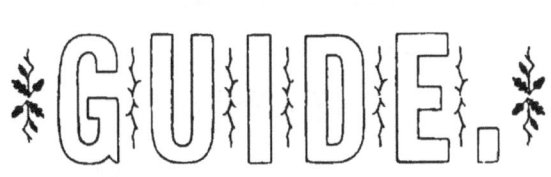

What Hotels to Patronize!
What Railways, etc., to Travel!
What Books and Papers to read!

COPYRIGHTED, 1885, BY
The National Gun Association,
Published Annually in June.
CINCINNATI, OHIO, U. S. A.

PREFACE.

These pages are designed to supply a long felt want, on the part of a large and rapidly increasing element of the American population, as well as of visiting foreign Sportsmen. An annual directory and guide such as this, will prove a welcome guest, not only to the stranger from abroad, but also, and more especially to our own sportsmen seeking knowledge, recreation and health. This book will not only aid them in finding such, but also in bringing before them in a condensed shape, where, *throughout the country*, they can purchase to the best advantage, the guns, ammunition, fishing tackle, dogs and equipments generally; where they can find the most congenial hotels; what roads of travel it will be best for them to pursue; in what sections they can hunt and fish to the best advantage; what books and papers pertaining to field sports they should read.

The support of all advertisers, in any way interested in this specialty, is especially invited, as is also that of all others, seeking to reach the now numerous community of sportsmen.

Respectfully,

The National Gun Association,

Box 1292. **CINCINNATI, O.**

To The Trade and Advertisers Generally!

We hereby respectfully call your attention to this publication, whose purport is indicated by the title. Arrangements have been made to place this volume on sale, through all the News Co.s, and their 17,000 Sub-Agents. As an advertising medium for your business, it will have no superior, as it will be in request by those parties whom you especially wish to reach. We solicit your advertisement with confidence, as the profits therefrom if any, will redound to the interest of a worthy Association.

Rates per Edition of 1885.

Full page, this size, 7x4 inches, $10.00; one-half page, $5.00; one-quarter page, $2.50; one-eighth page, $1.50; per inch of 12 lines Nonpareil Type, $2.00; per card of ½ inch x 2 inches, $1 00.

Guaranteed Circulation, 5000.

First complete edition will be printed June 1, 1885. Published annually as an addendum to The National Gun Association Hand Book, containing History Constitution, Trap Shooting Rules, etc.

SUMMER RESORT HOTELS—TAKE NOTICE:
HOTEL TRAP-SHOOTING.
(From Forest and Stream, N. Y. City, March 12, 1885.)

Editor Forest and stream:

While traveling last Summer in the West, I found a summer resort hotel in Michigan which afforded its guests a new and seemingly popular amusement in the shape of trap-shooting at clay pigeons. At the suggestion of some of the boarders, the hotel porter was induced to buy a trap and a few pigeons, and hire one gun, which he let the guests use at a certain price per shot. He soon found it so profitable that he bought several guns and more traps, finding it a paying investment during the whole season, shooters coming from all the neighboring hotels to participate. Is it not surprising that many of our summer resorts have not added glass-ball and clay-pigeon shooting to their old worn out list of amusement? The investment would not be large; say two guns at $35 each, two traps at $7 each, clay pigeons at from two to two and a half cents a piece. At a charge of five cents per shot or ten shots for forty cents, I have no doubt a paying business could be done, to say nothing of the amusement, which would be very attractive. The increasing interest shown in trap-shooting and field sports among gentlemen of the present day would soon make popular any hotel offering such amusement. Many a weary day have I spent on the seashore where snipe were said to frequent, waiting for the wind to blow ' sou'west." Something in the way of trap-shooting would have been a godsend. Let some of the humbugs advertising "good shooting and fishing" as an inducement for people to come to their places, provide clay-pigeon shooting for "off days," when the wind don't blow from the right quarter, and they will find their patrons much happier, and their own pockets better filled by the experiment. BEDFORD

BROOKLYN.

SPORTSMAN'S EMPORIUM,

538 WASHINGTON STREET,

SAN FRANCISCO, CAL.

LIDDLE & KAEDING,

Guns, Rifles, Pistols,

Ammunition, Fishing Tackle, Fancy Bait, Etc.

WHOLESALE AND RETAIL.

Sole Pacific Coast Agents for the Ligowsky Clay Pigeons and Traps.

—THE—
AMERICAN FIELD.

THE SPORTSMEN'S JOURNAL.

PUBLISHED WEEKLY.

Thirty-two pages, and containing the choicest reading matter on the GUN, RIFLE, ROD, DOG, HUNTING, NATURAL HISTORY, and all subjects pertaining to field sports and to travel and emigration of any paper published.

One Year, - - - - - $5 00
Six Months, - - - - 2 75
Three or more (Club Rates), $4 00 each, a year.
Single Copies, - - - - 10 Cents.
Foreign Postage, - - - $1 56 a year.

FOR SALE BY ALL
Newsdealers in the United States,
CANADA AND EUROPE.

ADDRESS ALL COMMUNICATIONS

AMERICAN FIELD PUBLISHING CO.,
243 STATE STREET, CHICAGO, ILL.
EASTERN OFFICE, 252 BROADWAY, NEW YORK.

ODOR OF FOREST! SPARKLE OF STREAM!

Do you own a gun, or a "fish-pole," or "bird-dog," or rifle? Ever go angling, or shooting, or tramping, or camping, or canoeing, or yachting? Have you a taste for studying the habits of wild birds and animals? Do you know that for ten years we have been publishing a bright weekly paper devoted to these subjects? It will repay you to look at a copy of the *Forest and Stream*. There is no other paper in the world just like it.

$4.00 Per Year; $2.00 for Six Months; Specimen Copy, 10 Cents.

Enter your Dog's Pedigree in the

AMERICAN KENNEL REGISTER,

Published monthly. Has already pedigrees of 2,200 dogs.

We publish

WOODCRAFT,
A Book for Campers, $1.

DOG TRAINING,
By S. T. Hammond, $1.

ANTELOPE AND DEER,
By Judge J. D. Caton, $2.50.

ANGLING TALKS,
By George Dawson, 50 cents.

CANOE AND BOAT BUILDING FOR AMATEURS,
By W. P. Stephens, $1.50

CANOE HANDLING,
By C. B. Vaux, $1.

CRUISE OF THE AURORA,
y Dr. C. A. Neide, Secretary American Canoe Association, $1.

And a
LIST OF OPEN SEASONS FOR FISH AND GAME.
10 cents.

ADDRESS:

FOREST AND STREAM PUBLISHING CO.

No. 39 Park Row,

NEW YORK CITY.

(ESTABLISHED in 1865.)

The Standard Authority.

The Turf, Field and Farm has the Largest Circulation of any Paper of its Class in America

Office of Publication for the **American Stud Book,** and **Chester's Complete Trotting and Pacing Record.** Acknowledged and endorsed by Turfmen and Breeders as the only Correct and Standard Authorities.

AMERICAN STUD BOOK (BRUCE), 4 vols.	$35 0
CHESTER'S COMPLETE TROTTING AND PACING RECORD	10 0
THE HORSE IN THE STABLE AND FIELD (STONEHENGE)	3 0
FIELD, COVER AND TRAP SHOOTING (BOGARDUS)	2 5
THE HORSE-BREEDER'S GUIDE AND HAND-BOOK	2 5
THE DOG—BREEDING, BREAKING, CONDITIONING (HUTCHINSON)	3 0
PRACTICAL HORSE-SHOEING (FLEMING)	7
THE COMPLETE 2:30 TROTTING AND PACING LIST	1
THE GUN TRIAL AND FIELD TRIAL RECORDS OF AMERICA	2
THE TROTTING HORSE OF AMERICA, HOW TO TRAIN AND DRIVE	2 5
RACING RULES	5
TROTTING RULES	2

The TURF, FIELD AND FARM has by far the largest circulation, and is the best general advertising medium of any paper o its class published in America.

Its enterprise, acknowledged ability, independent and gentlemanly tone, have made it the leading TURF journal, and a recognized authority on SHOOTING and FISHING topics and all manly and useful pastimes.

Newsdealers throughout the world have the TURF, FIELD AND FARM on sale.

Specimen Copies and List of Books sent upon application. Address

Turf, Field and Farm Association,

39 and 41 Park Row, New York

The Best and Cheapest Sporting Paper

IN THE COUNTRY.

PUBLISHED WEEKLY

At 5 Cents per Copy, or $2.25 per Annum.

Contains all the News, Hunting and Fishing, Base Ball, Billiards, Cricket, Turf, Athletic, Aquatic, Dramatic and Bicycling Departments.

COMPLETE RECORD OF ALL SHOOTING EVENTS.

Office, 202 South Ninth Street,

PHILADELPHIA, PA.

For Sale by all Newsdealers.

Sportsmen's and Tourist's
GUIDE BOOK AND MAP
—OF THE—
Dead River Region
OF MAINE.

Including valuable information in regard to the following FAMOUS FISHING RESORTS:

TIM and the SEVEN PONDS,
Rangeley Lakes
— AND —
LAKES MEGANTIC and SPIDER in CANADA.
— ALSO —

Descriptions of numerous other Ponds. "Hints on Camping." Routes, Hotels, Guides, Expresses, etc., etc.

PRICE (Postpaid) 50 Cts.

A. W. ROBINSON,

33 Winter Street, - - - BOSTON, MASS.

A NEW POCKET MAP OF THE
Rangeley Lake and Dead River Regions,
OF MAINE,

Designed especially for Sportsmen,

PRICE (Postpaid) 25 Cts.

A. W. ROBINSON,

33 Winter Street, - - - **BOSTON, MASS.**

PURE TOBACCO! PURE PAPER!
SPORTSMAN'S CAPORAL,
The Latest and becoming very popular.   Manufactured by special request.
A delicious blend of choice Turkish and Virginia.

STANDARD BRANDS: **SWEET CAPORAL,**   **CAPORAL,**
                                 CAPORAL ½,   **ST. JAMES ½.**
Straight Cut in FULL DRESS Packages, &c., &c.

KINNEY TOBACCO CO.,   *Kinney Bros.*
Succesors to Kinney Bros., NEW YORK.
Each Cigarette bears Kinney Bros.' fac-simile signature.

THE NATIONAL GUN ASSOCIATION.
Handicap Card.

For Matches announced in .... Prog., Ext. ....
Name...
Address..
Date.............................. Day...............
Permanent Handicap: Clay Pigeons ....
                 "   Live Pigeons ....
Tem. Handicap 1st Day Clay Pigeons .... yard .... day.
                "   2d   "   "   "
                "   3d   "   "   "
                "   4th   "   "   "
                "   5th   "   "   "
Shooters step in .... yard .... day.
Has he a previous record ? ....
Annual dues paid until.........................
Date.................... 18
.... Sec'y Nat. Gun Ass'n.
(Countersigned)
.... Chief Exec. Officer.

THE NATIONAL GUN ASSOCIATION.
Winners' Card.

Place...
Date..
No. of Programme Match...............................
    "   "   Extra   "   ....
Page of Score Book No.................................
Name of Winner.......................................
Number of Entries....................................
Entrance fee...
Deduct   per cent .... Money, being ...... %
Entitled to .... for .... Extra Birds.
Less ....
.... Scorer.
Paid.
.... Executive Officer.

MIXTURES FOR PIPE OR CIGARETTE.

THREE KINGS, Turkish Perique and Virginia.

MELLOW MIXTURE, Turkish and Perique.

TURKISH AND VIRGINIA.

PERIQUE AND VIRGINIA.

GENUINE TURKISH.

——— FLAKE CUTS, ———
Especially Adapted for the Pipe.

VANITY FAIR.   **OLD GOLD.**

BLACK AND TAN.

Fragrant Vanity Fair and Cloth of Gold Cigarettes.

ALWAYS FRESH, CLEAN AND SWEET.

Our Cigarettes were never so fine as now, they can not be surpassed for purity and excellence. Only the purest rich paper used.

13 First Prize Medals.   WM. S. KIMBALL & CO.

CALIFORNIA PATRON
→ AND ←
AGRICULTURIST,
No. 40 California Street,   SAN FRANCISCO.

J. CHESTER, Manager and Editor.

16 PAGES. 12 x 16.

THE CALIFORNIA PATRON

Was established in 1875, by authority, and under the directions of the California State Grange, as a farmers' journal, owned and controlled by the farmers of the State of California, and has been wholly devoted to the interest of the farm and the grange. It has maintained the reputation of the Farmers' Exponent and Advocate, and has been so well received and appreciated that its circulation has nearly doubled during the last year.

It was run as an eight-page monthly until 1878, when it changed to a semi-monthly, and run as such until March 6 1880, when it appeared as a Weekly. On the 1st of January, 1882, its size was increased nearly one-half. On the 28th of October, 1882, its size was again increased. On the 13th of September, 1884, it was again increased to a Sixteen-page paper, cut and stitched, and the Seventh increase was made January 1, 1885, to the present attractive size.

PUBLISHED WEEKLY,

Von Lengerke & Detmold,
14 Murray Street,   NEW YORK,

SOLE AGENTS
AMERICAN
WOOD-POWDER

NEW YORK SALESROOMS,

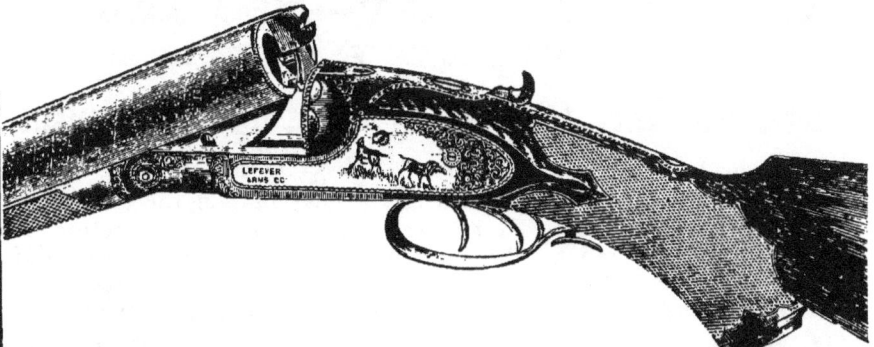

Lefever Arms Co.

IMPORTERS AND JOBBERS OF
GUNS, AMMUNITION
—AND—
GENERAL SPORTSMEN'S GOODS.

At the Second International Clay Pigeon Tournament, held at New Orleans, La., Feb. 11 to 16, 1885, the First Prize and Diamond Badge in the International Individual Championship Match, open to all the world, was won by B. Tiepel, with a Parker Gun. Among the contestants shooting other guns, were such champions as Carver, Bogardus, Cody, Stubbs, Erb, and others. During the entire tournament more prizes were won with Parker Guns, in proportion to the number used, than with any other gun.

New York Salesrooms, 97 Chambers St.

PARKER BROTHERS,
MAKERS,
MERIDEN, - - - - - - MASS.

C. C. C. & I. R'y---Bee Line.
REDUCED RATES
TO THE
Inter-State Shot Gun Wing Shooting Tournament,
At Springfield, O., May 5 to 9, 1885.

Parties paying full fare from any local point on the BEE LINE to attend the Shooting Tournament, will, upon presentation of certificate duly signed by the secretary of association, be returned at one cent per mile. Parties coming from Boston, New York, Buffalo and intermediate points, will have the advantage of through cars, via B. & A., N. Y. C. & H. R. R. and L. S. & M. R'y, and will land in the heart of the City of Springfield.

This is the only line with solid trains passing through the heart of the City of Springfield and is the Short Line between Cincinnati and Springfield, and has seven trains a day each way between these cities, and four trains a day between Cleveland and Cincinnati; and is the only line with through sleeping cars between Boston, New York and Cincinnati, passing through Springfield.

A. J. SMITH,
   GEN'L PASSENGER AGENT,
      Cleveland, O.

J. E. REEVES,
   GEN'L SOUTHERN AGENT,
      Cincinnati, O.

THE SPENCER REPEATING SHOTGUN!

WILL FIRE SIX TIMES IN THREE SECONDS,

Without Removing the Gun from the Shoulder.

THE BEST SHOOTING GUNS IN THE WORLD!

They have won the Connecticut Individual Championship Badge for 1884 Eight times, entitling winner to possession. They also won the Connecticut Team Championship Badge for 1884.

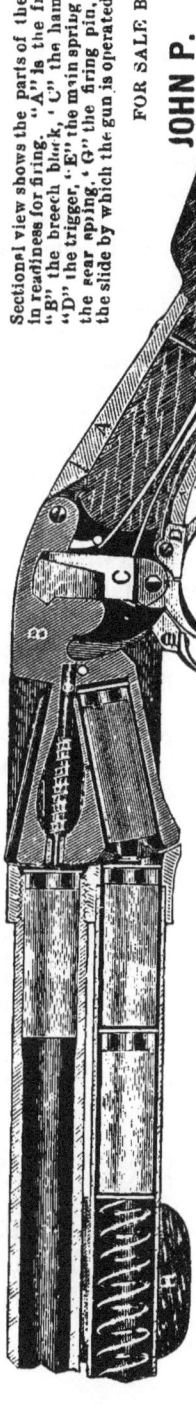

Sectional view shows the parts of the gun in readiness for firing. "A" is the frame, "B" the breech block, "C" the hammer, "D" the trigger, "E" the main spring, "F" the rear spring, "G" the firing pin, "H" the slide by which the gun is operated.

FOR SALE BY

JOHN P. MOORE'S SONS,

302 BROADWAY,

New York City.

The Magazine is located under the barrel and contains Five cartridges while one may be placed *in the barrel*. The backward movement of the slide on the magazine by the left hand, opens the breech, throws out the exploded shell and cocks the hammer. The forward motion puts a loaded cartridge into the barrel and closes the breech. After a little practice, this motion becomes intuitive, and six shots can be fired as rapidly as desired.

SEND FOR CIRCULAR TO **THE SPENCER ARMS CO., Windsor, Conn., U.S.A.**

THE PATENT MERINO ELASTIC FELT
GUN WADS

Should be shot by every first-class sportsman in the country. We have thousands of testimonials from prominent shots pronouncing them the best they ever used. By the use of these wads, your gun will give a better pattern and greater penetration than by the use of any other on the maket.

The hard unyielding wads, such as pink edge, black edge, or Baldwin, answered the purpose when they were first introduced, in the days of muzzle loading, cylinder barrels, but are not suited for breech-loaders; your choke bore gun, No. 12 gauge is 12 at the breech but 14 at the muzzle, you will find it so stamped on the barrels; then in a 12 brass shell, you put two, or three, or even more hard unyielding No. 10 pink edge, black edge, or Baldwin wads; now attempt to drive two or three No. 10 wads through your 14 muzzle gun, and you can form some idea of the strain you are subjecting your gun to, a strain that was never contemplated, and which accounts for the excessive recoil of breech loaders, their soon becoming shakey, and a majority of the bursted barrels of fine guns. Three evils that are entirely obviated by the use of our wads, which being elastic, give a uniform resistance from the breech to the muzzle, lessens the recoils causes the gun to shoot harder, and removes all danger of injury to your weapon.

Many of the largest Wholesale Firms in the United States are carrying a large stock, and recommending our goods to their trade, which is a guarantee of their merit.

Ask your nearest dealer for a box, or if he will not procure them, send stamps or postal note to us and we will mail you, postage paid, at the following scale of prices:

Standard, 3-8 Felt, 256 per box.	Second-grade, Thin Felt, for Shot, 256 Wads.
13 to 14 .... 35c. per box.	13 to 40 .... 25c. per box.
11 to 12 .... 40c. "	9 to 12 .... 25c. "
9 to 10 .... 40c. "	7 to 8 .... 30c. "
7 to 8 .... 50c. "	5 to 6 .... 30c. "
5 to 6 .... 60c. "	2, 3 & 4 .... 35c. "
2, 3 & 4 .... 65c. "	

THE PATENT MERINO ELASTIC FELT GUN WAD CO.

E. A. SHARRETTS, Secretary.

Factory, 41 W. Pratt Street,

P. O. BOX 307. **BALTIMORE, MD.**

BOGARDUS SAYS

"Clay Pigeons are by far a Superior Article for the sportsman, the use of which perfects one rapidly as a wing shot."

LIGOWSKY STANDARD
CLAY PIGEONS AND TRAPS.

(PATENTED).

No Country Home Complete Without This Popular Out-Door Sport.

Ready For The Healthy Entertainment Of Guests At a Moment's Notice.

SOMETHING NEW——"THE TONGUELESS LEVER."

(PATENTS PENDING).

Adapted and licensed solely for application to any Ligowsky Trap now in use, for throwing the "Tongueless" Ligowsky Clay Pigeon. Price, $3.

These Artificial Targets were used at

THE FIRST INTERNATIONAL CLAY PIGEON TOURNAMENT,
Chicago, May, 1884.

THE SECOND INTERNATIONAL CLAY PIGEON TOURNAMENT,
New Orleans, Feb. 1885.

And the Principal Inter-State Tournaments held in this Country since 1881. They are likewise used by the Champion Shots of the Country in their Individual Championship Matches, and have been adopted by the National Gun Association.

Constitution For Forming Gun Clubs, Furnished on Application.

WARNING: Buy or use no Clay Pigeons (or similarly thrown targets) or C. P. Traps, excepting those made by us. We own the original patents on Clay Pigeons (and similarly thrown targets) and Clay Pigeon Traps (and similarly throwing traps) Others are manufacturing in infringement of these patents, and all who use or sell such infringing Targets or Traps will be prosecuted. If you purchase any such, take a written guarantee from RESPONSIBLE parties, holding you free from liability.

For further particulars, rules and testimonials, apply to

THE LIGOWSKY CLAY PIGEON CO.,

P. O. BOX 1292.   CINCINNATI, O., U. S. A.

PITTSBURGH FIRE ARMS CO.'S HAMMERLESS GUN,
ANSON & DEELEY SYSTEM.

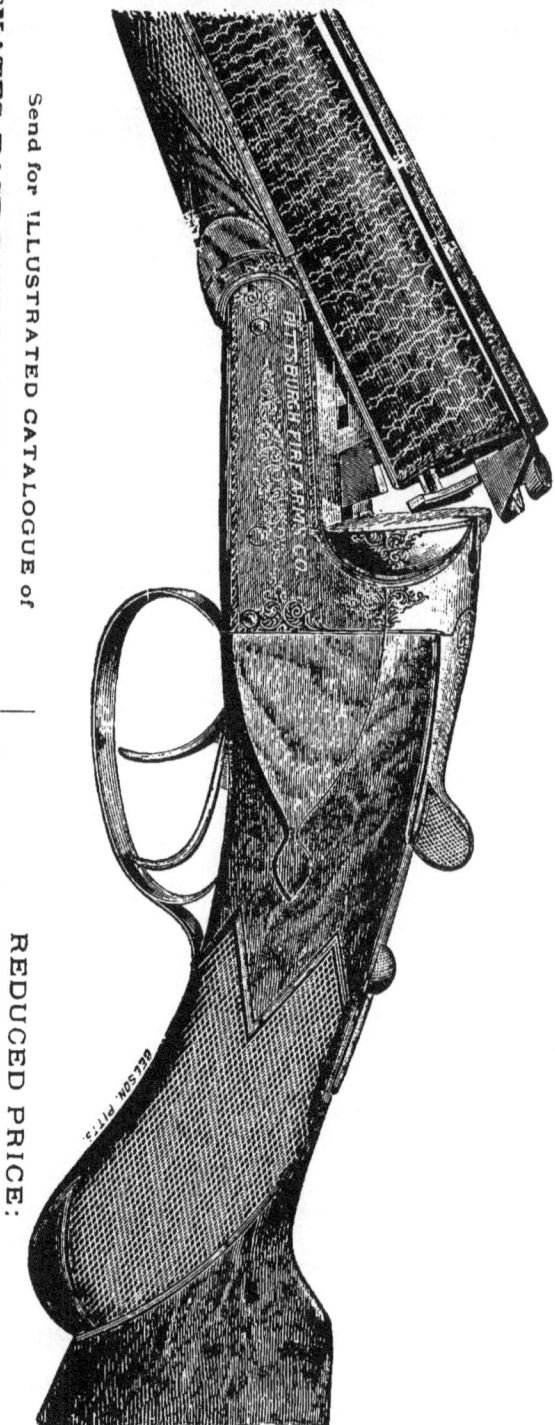

Send for ILLUSTRATED CATALOGUE of
SKATES, BASE BALLS & GYMNASIUM GOODS.
Sole Agents for the
Columbia and Victor Bicycle.

REDUCED PRICE:
2 Bore, $100.00;
10 Bore, $110.00.

166 FIFTH AVENUE,
PITTSBURGH, PA.

THE CHAMBERLIN CARTRIDGE CO.

CLEVELAND, OHIO,

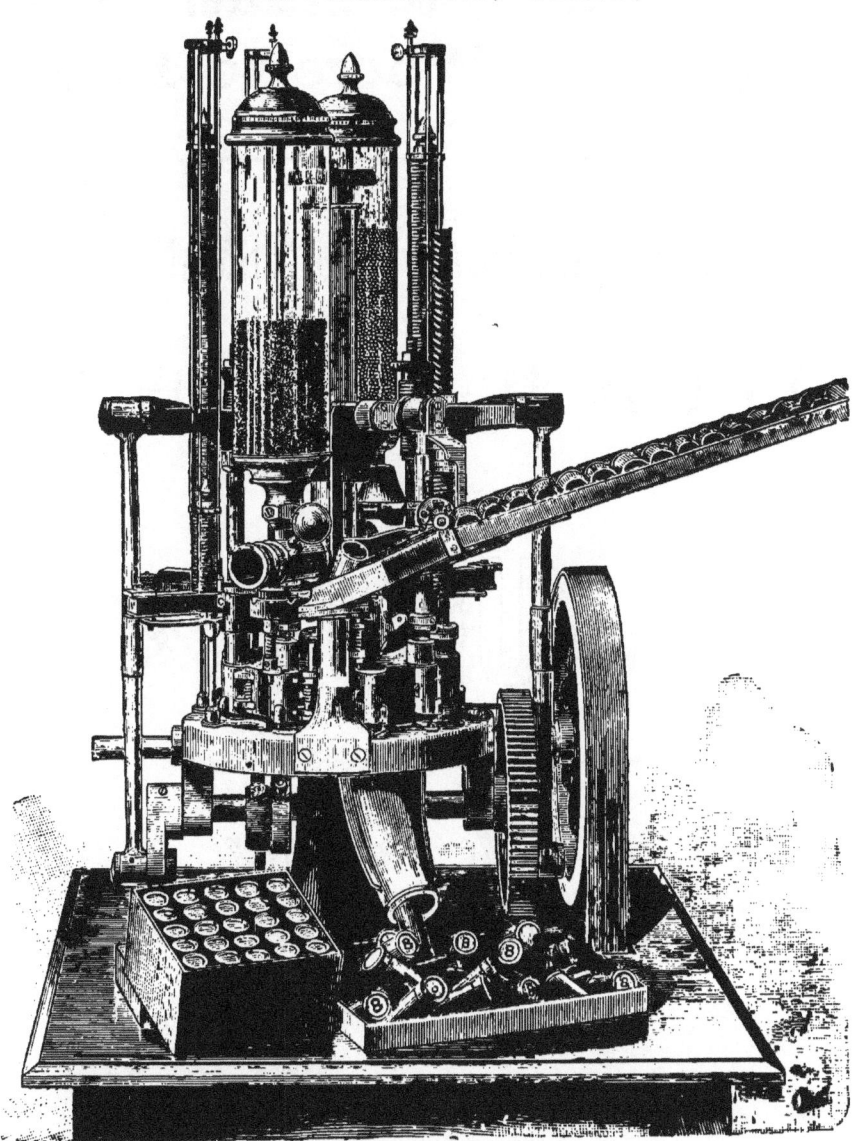

MANUFACTURERS OF

Fixed Shot Gun Ammunition,

Superiority in Uniformity, Convenience and Lower Prices.

Where to Buy!
Where to Hunt!
Where to Fish!

THE AMERICAN SPORTSMAN'S
DIRECTORY
—AND—
GUIDE.

What Hotels to Patronize!
What Railways, etc., to Travel!
What Books and Papers to read!

COPYRIGHTED, 1885, BY
The National Gun Association,
Published Annually in June.
CINCINNATI, OHIO, U. S. A.

www.ingramcontent.com/pod-product-compliance
Lightning Source LLC
Chambersburg PA
CBHW032239080426
42735CB00008B/922